GOSPELER

GOSPELER

Turning Darkness to Light,
One Conversation at a Time

WILLIE ROBERTSON

W PUBLISHING GROUP

AN IMPRINT OF THOMAS NELSON

ISBN 978-1-4003-3848-1 (softcover)
ISBN 978-1-4003-3849-8 (ePub)
ISBN 978-1-4003-3850-4 (audiobook)

Library of Congress Control Number: 2023941252

Printed in the United States of America
24 25 26 27 28 LBC 5 4 3 2 1

TABLE OF CONTENTS

Introduction: Faith Feller vii

PART 1: MY GOSPEL STORY

1. Swamp Dweller 1
2. Family Impeller..21
3. Broke Propeller 36

PART 2: THE GOSPEL STORY

4. Storyteller 61
5. Grace Rappeler 84
6. Bible Detailer 103

PART 3: RESPONSE TO THE GOSPEL STORY

7. Sin Cellar..125
8. Interstellar 144
9. Retailer...162
10. Hope Yeller.. 184

Notes 205

About the Author 207

But how can they call on him to save them
unless they believe in him?
And how can they believe in him if they
have never heard about him?
And how can they hear about him unless
someone tells them?

ROMANS 10:14 (NLT)

Introduction

FAITH FELLER

BEFORE YOU JUMP INTO THE FIRST CHAPTER, I WANT TO TAKE A MINUTE to introduce the concept of this book. Plain and simple, I am a Gospeler, and I want you to be one too. Perhaps you've never heard of the word *Gospeler*—I hadn't either until I began writing this book and was searching for just the right title. But as soon as I heard it, I knew a Gospeler is exactly what I have always aimed to be. The word is defined simply as "a person who zealously teaches or professes faith in the Gospel."[1] As a follower of Jesus, I believe we are all called to be Gospelers, and within these pages I hope to give you some tools to live like one. (Also, if you are wondering how to pronounce this word, here's a clue—it rhymes with the chapter titles—or as best we could.)

I have loved sharing the Gospel with people for as long as I can remember. It was something I saw in my home growing up and something that I hope to pass on to the next generation in our family, and this book is my attempt to pass it on to you. I believe that most people want to share their faith. The desire is there, but they believe that they just don't know how. In these pages I will present the way I have shared the Gospel with folks for many, many years, long before you may have known of me from *Duck Dynasty*. I began as a Gospeler in my teen years over takeout pizza and landline phones. I have shared what you are about to read with everyone from blue-collar guys in a deer stand to pro athletes in their hotel rooms. I've used a Sharpie on a napkin at a coffee shop and a marker and whiteboard at a church. I've shared with people you will never hear of and guys you may have watched in a movie last month. The bottom line is I hope by the end of this book you will be ready to share the Gospel with anyone who needs to hear the message that Jesus loves them enough that He came to earth for them, died for them, and was buried and raised so they might have the gift of eternal life and live with Him forever. That's the Gospel in a nutshell. And who needs to hear it? Everybody.

To be honest, I never thought about presenting my take on this message to others in this way until someone approached me with the idea at a conference after watching me walk a group through the main points of what you're about to read in this book. I'm sure you won't be surprised that I tell you some crazy stories in these pages. But I also offer examples of how I've shared the Gospel and give you an explanation of *why* as much as *what*. Trust me, I'm no pastor or theologian, but that's the point. If *I* can do this, *you* can too. All you have to do is care about people and want to give them an opportunity to hear the Good News. That's why this book isn't about training as much as transformation. Yes, I give you a method, but it's really about the message.

I'm around so many people who want to share the Gospel with others, but they often reveal that they have no idea where to start. I will give you a few great starting texts that have been life-changing for many people I've talked to over the years. I've noticed that breaking a big book down to a good starting point does wonders for people who find the Bible hard to understand and incorporate into their lives.

You might disagree with some of the things in this book, and that's fine. Sometimes we, as Christians, sit around and argue about the Bible. I'll bet if we spent that time focusing on people who obviously need to know the Savior instead of yelling at one another, we could do a whole lot more for growing the kingdom of God. Jesus left His followers with a Great Commission to go to all the world and make disciples. He told them to baptize them in the name of the Father, Son, and Holy Spirit and teach them everything He had commanded (Matthew 28:16–20). That's what I'm trying to do here on this earth—to help the lost be found, to bring those spiritually dead to new life, to take light into the darkness. And it begins with a conversation.

Bottom line: we cannot neglect the power of the Gospel in a world that is desperately searching for truth—now more than ever. My goal in these pages is simply to inspire, inform, challenge, and motivate you to share the Good News with the people around you. There are folks I could never reach—that your pastor or priest will never reach—but you can!

So climb up into a deer stand, pull up a chair at a coffee shop, or have a seat in my den with me as we open our Bibles and talk about the best news the world has ever heard—the Gospel of Jesus Christ!

> But in your hearts revere Christ as Lord. Always be prepared to give an answer to everyone who asks you to give the reason for the hope that you have. But do this with gentleness and respect. (1 Peter 3:15)

Part 1

MY GOSPEL STORY

One

SWAMP DWELLER

IN 2022, A SURVEY FROM ANCESTRY.COM REVEALED THAT MORE THAN half of Americans can't tell you the names of all four of their grandparents.[1] Yeah, I said their grandparents. Just two generations back. That survey showed me that most people today have very little connection to their heritage.

A while back, I became fascinated with my genealogy. Just the thought of everything that had to happen for me to be born in Bernice, Louisiana, on April 22, 1972, as the third son of Phil and Kay Robertson. (Bernice had the closest hospital to where my family lived in Arkansas at the time.) I learned about the people who played roles in my being born. I discovered that the further back you go in time, the more details can become lost. *People* can become lost.

Isn't it wild to think of being in some kind of magical room full of folks like your great-great-great-grandparents? Those are people you have never met or seen before, people you might not even like or want to be around. People who may be totally different from you, with different beliefs, maybe even coming from

1

opposing viewpoints. But if these folks didn't exist, neither would you! It blows my mind to think that if just one thing were different, if just one relationship didn't materialize, you wouldn't be on this planet. I'm glad everything worked out in my family, because it took all of them to get me and my biological children here. I'm also thankful my nonbiological children, my adopted and foster kids, are here. A whole different line of people had to come together to bring them into the world, to create the family my wife, Korie, and I have been blessed with.

ROBUSTO, ANDREA, AND LORENZO

My dad used to tell us we were of French descent. "Robicheaux, Robusto," he would say with a really lame French accent. Seemed to make sense. We are from Louisiana, so it could be true. But in reality, it's *not* true. I'm not sure who told him that, but I can guess that he loved the "Robusto" line. Sounds strong, right?

The people who helped my family research the Robertson ancestry sent me some exhaustive books on the history of our family line. According to the research, turns out we are not French after all. We are of Scottish-Irish descent. *Sorry, no Robusto, Phil!*

More recently, our family story took a wild twist with our reality TV show, *Duck Dynasty*. In one episode we went to Scotland to find our roots. And we did, in a crazy redneck sort of way. Knowing we had ancestors in that country, it was at least a good place to start. We traveled there based on a painting from the early 1500s that was in the National Galleries of Scotland museum. Two different friends on two separate trips to Scotland had come home and told me the same story: "There's a painting in a Scottish museum that looks exactly like you!" The crazy thing was, they were right. The guy in the painting looked just like me! (Seriously—google "Willie Robertson Scottish Painting.") Of course, we had to go over there and investigate, right?

It turned out the guy in the painting, Andrea Odoni, was not Scottish at all; he was Italian. He was not a long-lost relative; he wasn't even an important person or some noble like I had hoped. This piece of art is in a museum because of the fame of the painter, Lorenzo Lotto, not the guy in the painting. Wouldn't you know, by the time we traveled to Scotland to trace our ancestry and see this painting in person, it wasn't even in Scotland anymore! They had moved it to a museum in London. Like most *Duck Dynasty* episodes, the storyline was all mixed up, but hopefully it put some smiles on our viewers' faces. That said, Andrea Odoni did look just like me and happened to be a successful Venetian merchant. In the painting, he is clasping a small cross around his neck. Scholars say that represents Christianity taking precedence over pagan gods and nature. I like that symbolism, so at least there's that connection. Even if he wasn't some famous guy back in his day and it turns out we're not related at all, it's still pretty cool to have a painting that looks just like you.

I can imagine the smiles on the Robertson forefathers' faces if they found out their descendants were on TV. I guess first they would ask, "What's a TV?" They probably never even thought something like that was possible. Can you imagine if they found out our show was based on us running a duck-call business? Who would have thought!

In my book *American Entrepreneur*, I highlight businesses

and families who made fortunes and were some of the biggest names in America. Sadly, most eventually lost it all and were unknown within a few generations. Success doesn't necessarily get passed down. Fortune can last for a while, but fame sticks around for what seems like only five minutes—gone as quick as it came. Yet the same attributes that drove people to be successful in the first place are lost in future generations, because the next folks in line often have totally different life experiences than their parents or grandparents. Things come way easier for them, and ambition gets watered down or lost completely. They often don't have the same drive as those before them. Then someone else who is driven and hungry takes their place, and a whole new cycle begins for that generation.

> All people are like grass, and all their glory is like the flowers of the field; the grass withers and the flowers fall, but the word of the Lord endures forever. (1 Peter 1:24–25)

THAT ONE THING

I'm sure our family was able to experience some accomplishments that generations before us never thought possible. My dad's mother did make it on *The Price Is Right* when she was in her eighties and actually won *both* showcases. (Imagine an elderly Robertson woman running down the aisle after she heard, "Come! On! Down!") Because she got to be on TV, she was the most famous person I knew of in our family. I wasn't surprised at how well she did, because she *never* missed an episode. I know because I watched it with her until I went to kindergarten. But my grandmother would have had no idea what the future held for her family. That's the way life is. People pass away, sometimes never knowing what they actually hand down.

As I get older, I think more and more about what I will pass on. Truth be told, I wonder how long I have. I think we all have those thoughts. Business, money, and "stuff" seem to mean less and less the older I get. A lot of people my age start wondering if passing down a bunch of possessions helps or hurts those they leave behind. Did my motivation for business come from a place of having very little growing up? It's hard to know, but there weren't many material things passed down to me in the early days, that's for sure.

There is one huge thing passed on to me that I hope to pass on to our children. This is the one thing that affects every single part of my life. It has helped me in my career, my marriage, raising my children, with my friends, my travels, and pretty much everything in life. It didn't even require a family member passing away for something to be handed down to me. This one thing gives me joy when life gets tough, encourages me when I fail, offers me meaning and purpose. And best of all, it gives me hope for the future, and even beyond this life.

That one thing is the Gospel of Jesus Christ.

"And this is eternal life, that they may know You, the only true God, and Jesus Christ whom You have sent." (John 17:3 NASB)

That's what my mother and father desperately wanted to pass on above all else. Not even hunting or fishing was as important to our family as the Gospel. Dad was a gifted athlete but never pushed us into sports or tried to live vicariously through us. He wasn't opposed to athletics by any means, but it was definitely not a priority. I've seen enough parents at their kids' games, and I'm so thankful that mine didn't act like some of what I see these days. My dad, Phil, has a master's degree but never prioritized great grades or higher education. The priority was the Bible, the Gospel. There was no doubt what my parents wanted for us—the hope of Jesus Christ. Our priorities are faith, family, and ducks—in that order. (Ducks, for us, meant business, money, hobbies, and hunting, all rolled into one.)

Looking at our own family tree, it didn't take me long to find out how the Gospel was passed down. My spiritual 23andMe, if you will. Faith was fairly new to my mother and father; actually, it all really started for them just a few years after my birth. Although there were glimpses of faith in our family before my parents, my mother's parents were definitely not known for their spirituality.

For years, Dad had told me that I was named after a kid who failed his eighth-grade class three times named Willie Hunter. I think I was in the eighth grade when I found out that story wasn't true. Turns out I was actually named after my mom's father, Willie Ezell, who died long before I was born. An avid outdoorsman and workaholic, his life was never centered on God. My mother's father was around the age I am now when he passed away. He ran the family-owned general store in Ida, Louisiana, called Carroway's Grocery, which was in our family for over seventy-five years. My mom's dad rarely ever comes up in our family stories, even though we share the same name.

Maybe there aren't many memories of him because he passed away when my mother was young. His wife, my grandmother, who also died before I could really remember, had her own issues. After Willie's death, her life spiraled downward. She, too, wasn't rooted in anything spiritual. And so, when my grandparents on my mother's side are mentioned, it's usually in a very sad way.

Isn't that crazy that in just two generations someone can be almost completely forgotten?

Mom told me they were usually too busy working, so she went to church with her grandmother, Nanny. For my mom, Nanny was the one who passed down whatever faith she had in her. She was also the one who told my mom that someday my mom would have to fight for her marriage. This later proved to be true as well as critical to our Gospel genealogy. Nanny did pass on an important legacy. For that, she is never forgotten and is always an important part of our family's story.

My father's parents were Christians, but somehow this did not pass on to my dad. Whatever godliness he had witnessed in his life, he roundly rejected. Mom was a classic "good person" with no clue about what the Gospel really meant. So when they got married at a very young age, more out of necessity since they were going to have a child, things seemed to go south really fast.

Later on, I found out just how south things went and how close I came to *never* hearing about Jesus in my home. Sometime after I was born, my parents split up. My father was on the run, being hunted by the police for his part in a bar fight. In fact, for quite a while, he hid out in the swamps. But Dad wasn't homeless; he knew how to live in the wild.

Yeah, Phil was a swamp dweller.

In those days, our family was broke, so my mom, my two older brothers, and I had nowhere to live. All hope seemed lost. Had their marriage ended there, I could have experienced such brokenness and damage that I would never see, trust, or believe in *anything* other than the cruelty of this world. Thankfully, that's not what happened.

If I were to survey my own kids right now, I don't think any of them would even know their ancestors' names. However, had their ancestors' lives been filled with the Gospel, I bet I would have more to write about them and their lasting legacy. As it is, they might be a big part of my genealogy, but they are not part of my *Gospel* genealogy. That's a constant reminder to me to make sure I pass on what's truly important. I don't want to get caught up in all the stuff that seems like such a big deal in the moment but will simply be forgotten as time moves on.

Hope for our family arrived just in time in a very crazy way. Thankfully, the Gospel got through to my parents. And boy, did it ever show its power in their lives!

You see, at just the right time, when we were still power-less, Christ died for the ungodly. (Romans 5:6)

A SEAT AT THE TABLE

As I write this chapter, we're filming a major motion picture about our family titled *The Blind*. It's the story of how my parents' lives were drastically and radically changed by the Gospel. One day, I was on set watching the most surreal scene ever—my early life with my family being portrayed by actors and my two-year-old grandson playing me as a toddler. Sitting there watching faded memories vividly played out right in front of me, I was instantly taken back to my early days.

The Blind is a story of redemption, very real, raw, and, frankly, hard for me to watch. My church family has a phrase that is often shared: "Where you have no past, only a future." Well, that's true—unless they make a movie about it! While I'm glad other people will get to see the story of how Jesus dramatically changed our family, I don't have to watch the film to see what the Lord did with my parents. I don't need a movie to know how the Gospel changed the lives of me and my brothers for the better. I don't have to see it to believe it because I lived it all firsthand. I witnessed the beautiful plan of forgiveness and restoration that Jesus personified two thousand years ago.

I saw it. I felt it. And I am changed forever because of it.

When I visit with my parents at their home, I hear about more physical ailments than I ever knew existed. I can't help but notice all the medicine bottles on the dinner table, unsure if they are Mom's, Dad's, or a combination of both. I'm guessing mostly Mom's since Dad has never gone to the doctor much. But those meds sit on the same dinner table that we used to toss our bookbags on when we got home from school before we'd take our shoes off and run for the river to go fishing. The same table where we said a prayer every day before dinner and at the end of every episode of *Duck Dynasty*. The same table where I still remember my father telling us all we would one day sell a million dollars' worth of duck calls! Even though Dad might have been making somewhere around twenty grand a year at the time he said that, we all believed him and were excited for what was to come. He said all that at the same table where I watched Phil and Kay witness to so many people about the hope the Gospel offers.

I'll never forget all the times my dad sat there, looking right into a person's eyes and testifying with full confidence, "If there's a better way to get off this planet alive, I have not found one, other than what this Bible says."

With my parents getting older, I cherish all the moments we have together. I know a time will come when they will not be here for me to call up to ask a question about God's Word. Dad still grabs his Bible almost every time I'm there and reads passages out loud with the same wonder and passion as if he were reading it for the very first time. They're both still living out the commitment they made to the Lord almost fifty years ago. Dad is still preaching the Word every Sunday morning at a church and almost daily on his podcast, *Unashamed*, and Mom is still helping others, feeding people and reflecting Jesus in the way she loves others.

We all have a genealogy, but we don't all get offered a story like that. What a Gospel legacy I am a part of!

And so it was with me, brothers and sisters. When I came to you, I did not come with eloquence or human wisdom as I proclaimed to you the testimony about God. For I resolved to know nothing while I was with you except Jesus Christ and him crucified. I came to you in weakness with great fear and trembling. (1 Corinthians 2:1–3)

WRECKS AND RESTORATION

My dad's life BC, before Christ, was a whole different story. Phil was a "rank heathen," in his own words. Kay says he was "the devil." That probably says it all, right? Let's just say his life was not headed in the right direction. He was living the kind of life that ruins marriages, loses jobs, abandons kids, hurts people, and ends up wanted by the law—literally! He was the guy your parents taught you to avoid. Good people would be best advised to stay away from him. Dad was bad news, and he felt, at the time, that the worst decision he had made in life was to start a family and try to settle down. He had almost single-handedly destroyed everything around him. Mom had prepared to move on. He was a totaled vehicle hanging out with a bunch of others in the wrecking yard. At one point he'd shown lots of talent and promise, but now he was broken and wasted.

But the interesting thing about totaled vehicles is they are not actually unfixable—just deemed too expensive to repair. It's cheaper to just get another one than try to fix the original.

I had a truck that my son John Luke completely destroyed. He flipped it several times while driving with his friends, and it was considered totaled by our insurance. When I saw the truck after the accident, I agreed, "This thing is gone." I really loved that truck but was fine with selling it to the scrapyard, because the more important thing was that my son and his friends *weren't* totaled.

Crashes have a way of teaching valuable life lessons. Frightening and even life-altering moments have a way of reminding us what's really important. You hope in the moment that you get to live long enough to learn from the situation. Thankfully for us, everyone was safe. Life is precious—way more precious than a truck. Today, two of my grandchildren would not be here had it turned out worse. *Thank You, God!*

Several months later, a friend sent me a picture. I was totally shocked. The picture was of my truck! *Yep.* Not like the last time I saw it—crushed, bent, and totaled—but completely restored, back to how it looked in its prime. Maybe even better! See, this was no ordinary truck. The paint scheme was literally a one-off original. No other truck had that kind of custom paint job that made it stand out in the crowd. But there it was—my old truck made new.

Someone had seen the wrecked version of it on *Duck Dynasty* when we did an episode on John Luke's crash. Well, a guy in Arkansas saw something very different in that "totaled" truck: potential. He looked past all the twisted metal mess and made the trip from Arkansas to Louisiana to the scrapyard. For very little money, he towed it back to start the restoration—from an abandoned wreck in a junkyard to a restored truck getting to go down the road once again.

You can probably tell where I'm going here. That's the story of many of our lives, isn't it? It's easy to look at someone else the same way we look at a "totaled" vehicle. At some point they were careless, missed a turn or two, and found themselves careening out of control and into some barriers and got damaged. Thank God that He can see us beyond the external damage, just like that guy in Arkansas saw my beat-up truck. There is no cost too great to see us restored.

"The LORD does not look at the things people look at. People look at the outward appearance, but the LORD looks at the heart." (1 Samuel 16:7)

Now, back to my parents' story.

Phil and Kay Robertson's young family needed a miracle. One had already been shared with my dad in a honky-tonk in southern Arkansas. Of all the countless tales that had been told in that bar over the years, this one was different—this one was true, with the power to change the life of the person hearing it and the lives of everyone he knew. A miracle that could be exactly the good news needed for situations like this—a big ol' life mess that seemed hopeless, a totaled wreck in the scrapyard. That miracle had the potential to be the link to thousands upon thousands of future life changes and millions of people being influenced for God. The Gospel genealogy was primed and ready to explode in that tiny, rank watering hole in Nowhere, Arkansas. But it was almost missed.

Bill Smith was a local pastor at a church in Louisiana, which was about an hour's drive from that bar. I'm sure he never in a million years saw himself visiting the establishment. There was seemingly nothing there that would interest him. Men finding company with others who needed to drink away their sorrows was the exact opposite of the crowd he usually chose to be around. He led a church and preached a different way of dealing with life issues.

Bill was fiery. He knew the Bible but also had a strong compassion for the lost. He was breaking ground at a new church started by a group of families, led by a spirited young businessman who was becoming more and more successful in retail. That man was a World War II vet who came from nothing and was all about spreading the Gospel around the world. He was not a pastor but knew he could use his finances to grow the kingdom of God. He also loved music and was always singing. He and a group of believers had started a new church in West Monroe, Louisiana, and hired Bill to help grow the church, not just locally but with a vision and a mission to share the Gospel around the globe.

How would Phil Robertson, a young reprobate with no money, no real future, and no plans of helping anyone factor into the plans of Bill Smith and the church in West Monroe? Well, as it turns out, Phil's younger sister, Jan Dasher, was attending there. Her whole life, Jan was sold out for Jesus, and her devout faith certainly did not jive with Phil's choices. She had two goals: First, to get Phil to talk to someone about his life—just have a conversation. Second, to get the pastor to talk to her brother. What's crazy is, getting Phil to sit and talk to a pastor seemed much harder than the pastor going to the bar to talk to Phil! Phil would only go where he felt comfortable—and where he felt comfortable was on a barstool. The preacher would have to go to him. I can imagine that conversation going something like this:

JAN: "Pastor, will you talk to my brother about Jesus?"

BILL: "Sure, I'll talk to your brother. We can sit down after church."

JAN: "No, he ain't comin' to this church. You'll have to go to him."

BILL: "Okay, maybe we could meet for lunch?"

JAN: "No, you'll have to go to him . . . at his bar."

BILL: "Which bar in town is it?"

JAN: "No, his bar is out of state."

BILL: "Out of state? Wow. . . . Well, this *is* unusual."

A major spiritual timeline would hinge on all this coming together. But Bill agreed to go.

It's one thing to preach about the Bible, but it's another thing entirely to live your life according to the Bible. And Bill was living it out. He knew the Good News backward and forward from sharing it many times with many people. A lot of folks talk about spreading the Gospel around the world but have never even talked to their neighbor, much less made an hour drive to a run-down honky-tonk. The fact that he would go to a bar because one of his members asked was remarkable.

The pastor likely thought that my dad would probably never be a member of his congregation; he didn't even live in the same town. He wasn't going be a great giver to the church; he was broke. In fact, if everything went according to Bill's plan, Phil would even have to find a new job, because he owned and managed the bar. But this preacher knew his mission and was willing to share the Gospel, no matter what.

So, Bill got into his car and drove to find Jan's lost brother in the out-of-town, out-of-state bar.

Much like some ol' boy in Arkansas who saw a totaled truck and drove to Louisiana because he knew what it took to make it like new again, Brother Bill sensed something in Phil. Something no one else saw at the time, except his sister, Jan. He drove from Louisiana to Arkansas with hopes of restoring something that was totaled. Over the years he had seen a *lot* of wrecks that others had written off. But bottom line—Bill knew the power of the Gospel.

Years later, I talked to Bill about that fateful day. He told me how he walked into the bar and, just like Jan had said, there was Phil, sitting with a giant Budweiser in front of him. When Bill introduced himself, Phil sized him up, then asked, "What you sellin', preacher?" That's all the opening Bill needed. The Good News was preached, but on that day it seemed to miss the mark completely. There would be no crying, repenting, or falling on his knees. No barroom baptism. No spontaneous breakout of "Just

As I Am" would drown out the beer-drinkin'-and-cheatin' songs playing on the jukebox. Nope, after Bill had given his best shot, Phil just dryly said, "I'll keep that in mind."

Back to the same old miserable life.

But Bill knew that God only called him to be the messenger, to once again be faithful to go and share the story and explain the miracle of Jesus coming to earth and coming back from the dead. God was responsible for what the message could do in Phil. The seed had been planted.

I always wondered what that ride back to Louisiana was like for Bill. Was he talking to God, saying something like, "Well, Lord, that was an afternoon of my life that I'll never get back" or "I did my job; now You take it from here"? Did he have any idea what God was going to do with this family? Eerily prophetic, Jan told Bill and anyone who would listen about Dad, "You convert him, and he will convert a thousand." Jan has since passed away, but she was a Gospeler through and through. She never gave up on Dad, and God honored her faith and faithfulness.

I became a servant of this gospel by the gift of God's grace given me through the working of his power. (Ephesians 3:7)

ON A MISSION

Sadly for Phil, it took another run at awful living to spawn a remembrance of that Good News message. His life was like a truck out of control, crashing, rolling over and over, heading toward a terrible outcome. The miracle of the Gospel told in that bar seemed to be the furthest thing from Phil's mind. Sometimes, though, when we are so far away from God, the flicker of the Gospel light is like a beacon from a distant lighthouse showing the way home.

> SOMETIMES, THOUGH, WHEN WE ARE SO FAR AWAY FROM GOD, THE FLICKER OF THE GOSPEL LIGHT IS LIKE A BEACON FROM A DISTANT LIGHTHOUSE SHOWING THE WAY HOME.

Less than a year later, that miracle finally took hold. When Dad told Bill, "I'll keep that in mind," he did just that. Eventually Phil drove to Louisiana to make things right with Mom and hear more about the Gospel. He'd finally hit bottom, had enough of wrecking his life, and was ready to change.

Soon, the old Phil was slain in a watery grave, and a whole new man was born—born again! A real, biblical, spiritual miracle took place. I'm sure there were lots of people waiting to see if this change was going to take or not. I'm sure even my mom had her doubts. But that's exactly how seeds work. You plant them and wait to see if they grow.

"In the same way, I tell you, there is rejoicing in the presence of the angels of God over one sinner who repents." (Luke 15:10)

I was very young when my parents gave their lives to Jesus. My physical life, along with Phil and Kay's spiritual life, was on about the same timeline. And in that same time frame, Phil had the idea for Duck Commander. As I write this chapter, we just celebrated the fifty-year anniversary of Dad inventing his legendary duck call. I also just had my fiftieth birthday.

Growing up, I certainly heard about the "old Phil," but all my memories were of the new version, the fully restored model. I recall some moments when I could sense the tension in the house from the old life. But what I knew most was hearing Phil sit at our table and tell others about how he used to live, all while he would have his Bible open, teaching. I witnessed countless people, over and over, from all walks of life, going to the river by our house to be baptized after praying with Dad.

The man was on a mission to share his faith with whoever would listen—and some who wouldn't! I would go on trips with him as he sold duck calls. Always the same thing: he would demonstrate the various calls and then he would preach. *Always!* With me watching and listening, he was passing this down to me, sermon after sermon, Bible study after Bible study, person after person.

Growing up, I witnessed one of the greats *witness*.

As I look back on my heritage of a family living for the Gospel, I trace it back to that one moment, that one meeting at that bar in Arkansas. The start of the old joke, "A guy walks into a bar . . ." took on a whole new meaning with Phil and Brother Bill. That one guy who decided to take a chance on sharing his faith. That sister who would not give up on her brother and saw something there that he could not even see in himself.

Of course, it goes without saying that my mom giving her life to Jesus was transformative for our family as well! She went first. She became a Christian during the time she and Dad were separated. Mom and us boys started going to Brother Bill's church in West Monroe. Mom heard the Gospel and invited Jesus into her life. She had to be a quick disciple, because she would soon be asked to forgive all the sins Dad had blasted toward her and pretty much everyone else he knew. Dad was about to make an appearance back into our life story, now as a new man repentant and washed clean by the blood of Jesus.

All these events lined up to shape my life. It's strange to think how everything could have ended up so very differently. If the Gospel had only changed the lives of myself, my brothers, and our mom, it would have been worth it. Yet there was so much more to come once our whole family came to know Jesus.

I can't help but think how the Gospel dictated the way my life turned out in my relationship with my wife and the lives of our children and grandchildren. We all have the DNA of the Good News of Jesus in us because His fingerprints are all over everything we are and everything we have done. The lives of my siblings and their families, and all those who heard the message from Phil and Kay over these past fifty years, are forever changed because of the Good News. Changed because one man and woman acted on the Gospel.

There seem to be endless stories from folks all over the world who tell me, "I was at an event where your dad spoke about Jesus, and I was forever changed." That means new spiritual lineages cropped up all over, and it can all be traced back to a man who was God in the flesh, died on a cross, came back to life, and now sits at the right hand of the Father on our behalf (Hebrews 10:8–14).

Here on this earth, for our family, it all started with one man who got in his car and drove to a bar to tell a swamp dweller about his Savior.

GOSPELER

A restored life telling a totaled life how you can be rescued and redeemed.

For I am not ashamed of the gospel, because it is the power of God that brings salvation to everyone who believes. (Romans 1:16)

Two

FAMILY IMPELLER

HAVE YOU EVER CONSIDERED HOW YOU GOT WHERE YOU ARE? THOUGHT about all the people who allowed God to work through them to get you to today, even beyond your family? Looking at our culture, there are so many things that can negatively affect a family line and legacy, like divorce, disputes, disease, and death. But unfortunately, there aren't many things that change an entire family line for the better. Even events like winning the lottery, receiving a big inheritance, or getting your own reality TV show can turn out to be destructive and cause a family to be worse off than before. But when Jesus comes into a home, He can change everything forever. That's definitely what happened to us Robertsons.

My family's new life led us to move from rural southern Arkansas to the outskirts of West Monroe, Louisiana, where Bill lived. We also started going to the church where he preached. The change led my mom to do things like pack us boys up and drive to a nearby Christian camp when we had no money for the week's cost. When we got there, Mom told us to wait in the car while she went to find the director. After a while, she came back and said, "Okay, boys, they said y'all could stay." So, out of the car we ran to the cabins, while Mom walked to the dining hall.

Mom had asked the director if she could trade working in the kitchen all week for us to get to attend the camp. She wanted us to learn about Jesus way earlier in life than she and Dad had, hopefully to save us from the misery she had to live through. That week, we had a blast, while Mom was in the kitchen helping cook and clean up after three meals a day for a camp full of kids.

But there was more in store for me than Jesus that week. As a fifth grader at the camp, I would meet a young girl named Korie. I would get up the nerve to ask her on a moonlight hike, and she would agree to go. Korie also went to that same church Bill pastored. Remember in the last chapter when I mentioned a successful businessman who had funded the start of the new church and hired Bill? Well, that same man also put up all the money to build the Christian camp we went to that week.

And that same man was none other than Korie's grandpa, Alton Howard. Alton was instrumental in hiring Bill, who shared the Good News with my father. And now after thirty-plus years of marriage to Korie, I'm still in awe of what all took place to make this happen.

Yes, the Gospel is tethered to *all* of our story. The word *impel* used in this chapter's title means "to urge or drive forward . . . as if by the exertion of strong moral pressure."[1] From the day my parents came to Christ, Jesus has been our family's Impeller, the One who urges and drives us forward as our motivation and mission.

A PRAYER AND A PLATFORM

Duck Dynasty actually started with Korie. She had the idea for our family to do a reality TV show. Korie was the only one who had done any "research," because she was the only person in the entire Robertson family who watched reality TV! The conversation started something like this:

> **KORIE:** We should have a show about your family.
> **ME:** I don't really think we're that different from any other folks. We're just normal people.
> **KORIE:** Willie! Your family is *not* normal!

> *Well, she had me there.*
> *So, I drove down to the river to tell Phil*
> *about the idea of us doing a TV show.*

> **PHIL:** It will never work. Why would anyone watch *us*?

> *I didn't tell Dad that I had thought the same thing,*
> *how we were just a typical American family. But*
> *I did lay out why I thought we should try.*

> **ME:** It could be good for business.

Dad still didn't seem interested. That is, until I threw out . . .

> **ME:** We could pro'lly preach the Gospel to more people.

> *Phil cut his eyes up at me from his recliner.*

> **PHIL:** You think so?
> **ME:** I don't see why not!
> **PHIL:** Hey, if we can get the Gospel out to more people, I'm in.

Remember in chapter 1 when I said I grew up knowing our priorities were faith, family, and ducks—in that order? Well, the idea of our *family* being on TV didn't get Dad on board. Helping our business (*ducks*) didn't work either. But number one—*faith*—got his attention.

So that was it. Two short conversations led our family to a whole new venture—the crazy business of reality TV.

We decided a good ending for every episode of the show would be a dinner around our family table and, of course, a prayer. We never really thought this was something out of the ordinary. In fact, I didn't realize that most people *didn't* pray before their meals. I know those who do practice this were glad to see it on TV. We got messages from people all over the world about how those prayers meant so much to their families. I'm sure some had no idea what it even meant, while others may have remembered it from their past. But some actually started the practice after watching the show.

I think some families realized that they rarely all sat together for a meal anymore. Everyone eating on the run on their own because of busy schedules has become the norm. Setting aside a time not only to be thankful but to eat and share life together seemed to be something in the past for many people. But some of the best sermons I have heard were not from a pulpit, but at the family table.

That weekly ending with our prayer at dinner was broadcast into living rooms all over the world. Millions and millions were yet again influenced by the Gospel being shared with my parents as a couple in backwoods Arkansas. The times we sit together as a family and thank God are always a reminder to us that there was another time when we did *not* all sit together at a table. The times when we thought we would have one less person there—our dad—and the time in the history of our family when there was not a whole lot of good news. That family prayer is a constant reminder of everything God has done in our lives.

> Then Jesus told his disciples a parable to show them that they should always pray and not give up. (Luke 18:1)

THE LIGHT BEHIND THE SPOTLIGHT

Korie and I went on to have six kids in all sorts of interesting ways—having them ourselves, adopting, and just taking them in as our own. They have all kinds of gifts, skills, and talents. Each one has been touched by the Gospel, and like I always say, "I can't tell ya how they turned out, because they are still turning out." We are all constantly growing. And, for a few years now, our kids have begun having kids of their own.

Our daughter Sadie has a unique gift of communicating the Gospel to all sorts of people. In fact, the more people in the room, the more she excels. Since for most folks the fear of public speaking is ranked higher than the fear of dying, I would say her gift definitely stands out. Especially because she has done it since she was a teenager. She has millions of social media followers who are constantly exposed to the Gospel through the things she posts. Our other children also spread Jesus in different ways through their various jobs and giftings. This is one more example of fruit that came from someone taking a chance to go out and preach the Gospel, and now my own children are doing the same decades later. A real Gospel genealogy.

One of the questions we often hear is, "How do you guys stay faithful in the spotlight?" I think it's because of how grateful we are to God for bringing my parents out of an awful spot that almost claimed their marriage. The reason we talk about the Gospel is because without it we would not have any of the success we enjoy now. I'm certainly not saying that when you live for the Lord all your troubles will just melt away. This is not a prosperity gospel kind of book. I am saying there would literally not be a company called Duck Commander had the Gospel not intervened, which would mean there would be no *Duck Dynasty*; no books like this; no podcasts, TV appearances, or movies; no messages or sermons.

The spotlight we were given as a family was made available by finding *the* Light and living in the light (John 8:12). When there was no Gospel, life was horrible and dark. When the Good News entered the picture, light was actually created. I have always said if you see anything good in me, it's not because I am good at all; it's simply the Light I'm reflecting. If we didn't give the credit to God, we would not be telling the real story.

"While I am in the world, I am the light of the world."
(Jesus in John 9:5)

The reason I try hard to never give up on anyone is because Aunt Jan never gave up on her brother. Because Pastor Bill didn't give up on Dad. Because my mother, who had the most to forgive, didn't give up. Dad's story taught me that you never know what Gospel genealogy may be getting started when you take that chance and share God's plan to save His creation. It's not just His power to change lives that are trapped in wickedness but also the unlimited possibilities to help create new lives full of joy and hope.

The Gospel offers the peace of knowing no matter what happens here, there is life beyond this life. Knowing that truth alone can change everything; even death can be a victory, not a defeat. So I don't give up on people, because I know the power that is there to completely change lives, no matter how bad things may be. You may have someone in mind right now who needs life change. I hope for their sake you won't give up on them.

In a fallen world where human behavior can make you want to give up, the hope of the Gospel gives me strength to continue to share the story with others. In the first chapter, I talked about my Gospel genealogy in connection to my family. But once we are adopted into God's kingdom, that circle is expanded. As for me, I began to be influenced not just by my parents but by scores of other people who helped make me who I am today. We each have to take hold of the Good News for ourselves for the lineage to continue in our circles. That genealogy doesn't look like a normal family line. How many hundreds of people helped create my spiritual family tree? What about yours? Think of who came into your life at just the right moment to help you on your path.

I love how God calls Himself Father and the body of Christ a family—spiritual brothers and sisters, spiritual dads and moms. Where our natural family might come up short or even flat-out fail, God can create a new family. The ones who help start that path by sharing the Good News are always special; they are a part of your Gospel genealogy.

Even if you had ten thousand guardians in Christ, you do not have many fathers, for in Christ Jesus I became your father through the gospel. (1 Corinthians 4:15)

NAME ABOVE ALL NAMES

She will give birth to a son, and you are to give him the name Jesus, because he will save his people from their sins. (Matthew 1:21)

The most important name in any Christian's Gospel genealogy is the name *Jesus*. I don't think there has been a single day where His name has not been brought up in our family. Jesus comes up in happy times, sad times, times of need, times of confusion, all times, all the time. When I have great success, I am thankful to Him. When I totally screw up, I go to Him. When I run into others who are in a bad spot, I tell them about Him. On the earth thousands of years ago, halfway around the globe from where I am today, He did not speak the same language I speak. He was from a different culture, and if He walked in the room, I would likely not recognize Him. But I see Him in so many others' lives. And the people He hung out with during His life on earth are also constantly in my conversations. I read about Him over and over. I listen to others who talk about Him. There is no person in my ancestry whose name even comes close to being mentioned as much as the name of Jesus.

And just when I might think I have learned all there is to know about Him, I discover something new. I also get inspired by others who follow Him in all different walks of life all over the world. I am mesmerized by people who arrange their entire lives around Him—those who sacrifice all their worldly desires and ambitions for His name. I am awed by people who have laid down their lives rather than deny their faith in Jesus. We are part of a very powerful Gospel genealogy. Someone, somewhere passed this message on, over and over, because had they not, I would never have heard about it. For two thousand years, Gospelers have spread the message of hope without phones, internet, electricity, airplanes, printing presses, or anything we have today. Just by the power of the Gospel.

Over the generations, the spread of the Gospel has depended on only one thing—people who love Jesus telling others about Him.

"Therefore go and make disciples of all nations, baptizing them in the name of the Father and of the Son and of the Holy Spirit, and teaching them to obey everything I have commanded you. And surely I am with you always, to the very end of the age." (Matthew 28:19–20)

I will take my place in the long line of Gospelers. For a lot of folks I might be the closest thing to a preacher they will ever know. But I don't consider myself to be a Bible scholar. I don't work for a church. I'm a businessman. I'm not an official pastor, elder, or deacon, just a proclaimer of the Gospel, both publicly and personally.

I am a Gospeler.

To be a Gospeler, no résumé is needed, no particular skill set, and no gifted communication skills. My parents passed this on to me as the thing of first importance. The Gospel is what I take my stand on, to be heard by others and seen in the way we live our lives, because "in him we live and move and have our being" (Acts 17:28).

The Bible has genealogies listed throughout the Old and New Testaments to connect and confirm family lines that God worked through.

The reason that any genealogy is included in the Bible, and the reason I have placed one in this chapter, is because there is a big-picture purpose for us to understand the importance of a certain family line. For example, this list includes the generations of people who helped bring the Savior of the world to planet Earth!

Jesus, when he began his ministry, was about thirty years of age, being the son (as was supposed) of Joseph, the son of Heli, the son of Matthat, the son of Levi, the son of Melchi, the son of Jannai, the son of Joseph, the son of Mattathias, the son of Amos, the son of Nahum, the son of Esli, the son of Naggai, the son of Maath, the son of Mattathias, the son of Semein, the son of Josech, the son of Joda, the son of Joanan, the son of Rhesa, the son of Zerubbabel, the son of Shealtiel, the son of Neri, the son of Melchi, the son of Addi, the son of Cosam, the son of Elmadam, the son of Er, the son of Joshua, the son of Eliezer, the son of Jorim, the son of Matthat, the son of Levi, the son of Simeon, the son of Judah, the son of Joseph, the son of Jonam, the son of Eliakim, the son of Melea, the son of Menna, the son of Mattatha, the son of Nathan, the son of David, the son of Jesse, the son of Obed, the son of Boaz, the son of Sala, the son of Nahshon, the son of Amminadab, the son of Admin, the son of Arni, the son of Hezron, the son of Perez, the son of Judah, the son of Jacob, the son of Isaac, the son of Abraham, the son of Terah, the son of Nahor, the son of Serug, the son of Reu, the son of Peleg, the son of Eber, the son of Shelah, the son of Cainan, the son of Arphaxad, the son of Shem, the son of Noah, the son of Lamech, the son of Methuselah, the son of Enoch, the son of Jared, the son of Mahalaleel, the son of Cainan, the son of Enos, the son of Seth, the son of Adam, the son of God. (Luke 3:23–38 ESV)

I know a lot of those names are tough to pronounce, but they're all folks in Jesus' genealogy. Those are the people God used to get Him here. The One who provided the Good News has a bloodline that goes all the way back to the beginning.

And there are people right now who need to be brought into *your* Gospel genealogy.

ANYONE CAN

Now, here's some more good news—*you* can be a Gospeler too.

Your parents might not have been the ones who told you about Jesus. You may feel like the first in your Gospel genealogy. But to become a Gospeler, you have to overcome the excuses:

- It's just not my gift.
- There are people better at sharing their faith than me.
- I don't know the Bible well enough.
- I haven't even figured it all out myself, so how could I ever help someone else?

- With my past, I don't feel like I'm worthy to talk to someone.
- Isn't that what my pastor is for?
- (Insert your own excuse here.)

There are lots of reasons we come up with that hold us back. But I'm telling you, you can do it. The entire reason I wrote this book is to say, "You can do it!" If you can tell someone about your spouse, your kids, your school, your pets, or your hobbies, you can tell them about the most important thing in your life—your Lord!

So, let me stop here and ask:

Could you share the Gospel with another person?

Do you know what the Gospel is?

Would you know where to start?

Have you made sure that you have passed it down or are passing it down to your children?

If the answer is no to any of these questions, it's okay. Let's learn how to get better at it. Take this journey with me and give the best gift you could ever give to someone—the Good News of Jesus. Whatever may have held you back will be covered in these pages. It's not complicated. If I can do it, anyone can. The more you share, the easier it gets. The good news about being a Gospeler is that we're only called to do the sharing part. God is the one who grows it into faith.

Paul shared how God works in and through His followers to reach people:

I planted the seed, Apollos watered it, but God has been making it grow. So neither the one who plants nor the one who

waters is anything, but only God, who makes things grow.
(1 Corinthians 3:6–7)

Remember the story I shared about the painting in a museum halfway around the world that looked like me? The first time I was told about it, I really didn't pay much attention. I figured I wouldn't think it looked like me, and there was no way for me to know firsthand. But then I heard from another person the same exact story. Now I'd heard it from two *different* people who had known me a long time. Eyewitnesses saying the same thing.

So now I thought it was possible that it could be true. Telling a person that someone else looks like them is actually kind of bold, because that opinion can backfire and go all kinds of wrong. I know, because one time I told my wife she looked like a certain woman on TV, and she *totally* disagreed.

Had my friends known more information, like who painted the picture, or the guy who was in the painting, I probably would have just looked it up for myself, but all I heard was, "There's this guy in a painting in Scotland that looks just like you!" My second friend was so convinced that he went the extra mile by taking a picture on his phone. The truth became very clear when I saw it for myself. *Wow, it is me!* I was blown away! In fact, when I was meeting with the production company at my home about *Duck Dynasty* and they saw the picture, they asked if I had commissioned a self-portrait. *Yeah, that sounds just like something I would do, right?*

But what if my friends had not told me about it after they visited the museum? I would never have known that a famous painter had created this piece of art of a Christian business guy who resembled me. My family would not have gone to Scotland, and we would not have told the story on TV. Millions of people all around the world saw the episode, so had my friend not told me, that connection would have never been made. The story would never have been told to so many to see it for themselves.

So why do I bring this strange story back up?

Because it's a lot like how the Gospel is spread. Sometimes when it's shared, it just doesn't resonate, a lot like when my father first heard the story and just blew it off. But he would eventually redirect his entire life and help change the lives of many others because of that same story. It's kind of like planting a seed, as we just read in 1 Corinthians 3. At first, nothing comes up. But someone else comes along and adds just a bit of water and soon a green leaf pops out of the ground. Just like that friend's photo helped me realize what I failed to believe initially, when the Gospel is heard, accepted, and responded to, it's not just a cool story, but a game changer. A story like that can spread across the world!

> **WHEN THE GOSPEL IS HEARD, ACCEPTED, AND RESPONDED TO, IT'S NOT JUST A COOL STORY, BUT A GAME CHANGER.**

Regardless of your Gospel genealogy, your name can become a crossroads in your family line. I told you earlier how Jesus became our family's Impeller, how He alone is the One who urges and drives us forward in our calling to share the Gospel with the world. No matter your family background or the community you have been surrounded by, Jesus can become your motivation, giving your life this same purpose through His plan.

That's why I want to help you unlock the Gospeler in you. Let's learn how to be great seed-spreaders and watch how God can make them grow. Someday, somewhere, someone may owe their eternal destiny to you doing just that!

I pray that the sharing of your faith may become effective for the full knowledge of every good thing that is in us for the sake of Christ. (Philemon 1:6 ESV)

Three

BROKE PROPELLER

I GREW UP ON THE OUACHITA RIVER IN NORTHEAST LOUISIANA. WE moved there when I was around four years old. Dad was a commercial fisherman back then, so fish stories were always a big part of our family life. I have many great memories of living on the water. Usually once a year after some big rains, the river ended up in our yard, getting ever so close to the house. Not really *Avatar*—more like *Waterworld*, the 1995 Kevin Costner sci-fi classic.

The flood of 1991 overtook the little shack my grandparents lived in at the time. I used the unfortunate circumstances to impress my then-girlfriend Korie by paddling on a big chunk of Styrofoam through the house to retrieve family pictures that were still hanging on the walls. I'll never forget all the snakes that were trapped in each room that I had to navigate around and through. But my bravery must have worked, because Korie and I got married that winter. She was impressed.

It's funny, all the little things you remember from your past. When I go back down to that river today, it's amazing how quiet it is. It's like going back in time. The pace of life is very slow. Part of the reason is that the cell service is really poor, so there are no distractions out there. It's calming. The sounds of the city and busy traffic are replaced with birds singing and dogs barking. At night, all the insects and frogs take over with their powerful orchestra.

But there was one distinct sound I can remember hearing all the time growing up there. That's the screaming noise of big, fancy bass boats zooming down that river at full speed. You could hear those giant motors from way off, like a jet airplane getting closer. We could guess the size of the motor just by how it sounded. We noticed because all we had were these small, rinky-dink Evinrude or Mercury outboards that were never very impressive.

With boats, the motor supplies the power, but the propeller makes 'em go. Now, of course, you can't see the propeller, because it's under the water spinning really fast, pushing the whole boat. And on those big, expensive bass boats, people loved giving them as much gas as they could to make them go full bore.

Our little piece of the earth was right where Cypress Creek branched off the Ouachita River. Because there were so many old dead trees and stumps in the water that fish like to hang around, we had some great fishing. Some of the stumps you could easily see, but most were just under the water's surface. Awesome for fishing, but not so awesome for boat propellers. It's best to ease a boat through that creek the same way you would walk to the bathroom at night with all the lights off—slowly and cautiously!

As these guys raced down the river on their expensive boats, they would see the mouth of that small creek. Most would get curious and feel like they had to turn in to check it out. They would slow down slightly to make the turn and then go wide open. That's when you'd hear *that* sound—the collision of the propeller with a waterlogged stump. And the stump *always* won. Every time. With the propeller knocked out of commission, the motor would slow to a stop, and the boat would begin to drift. And us poor little barefoot river rats would yell out, "I hope you got a paddle!" While we didn't have nice, big boats, we did have the very valuable knowledge of where those stumps were!

There are two things you should know about broke propellers: First, it means the fun is over, because you're dead in the water until you get help. And two, it is *not* an easy fix.

Most of the stranded boaters ended up paddling to our place and borrowing the landline in our house to call for a ride. (This was obviously way back before cell phones.) They were usually broken down miles from where they put their boat in. There were no signs of any kind to warn folks to slow down, so you had to learn the hard way—the expensive way. There is a graveyard of propellers at the bottom of that creek.

To protect your boat, you need to enter the creek just like the pace of life there—very slowly. When you damage your propeller, you need help—pretty quickly. Same is true in life when you go too fast and hit a stump, so to speak.

STUMPS IN THE WATER

Throughout my twenties, I worked full time at Camp Ch-Yo-Ca. It was a fun time in life. Our children spent a lot of time there growing up. Over the years, we helped bring many young people closer to the Lord at that camp. Most of the year, I worked alone until the busy summers arrived and were filled with kids packed with energy that needed to be burned off. I loved the lake because I could teach about fishing while also teaching about God, and I can rig a cane pole faster than any human alive. I had to be quick because kids who are new at fishing constantly tangle their poles.

Because my in-laws owned the camp, I worked for my wife's family, and as I said before, they were very successful in business. I remember whispers from some people with questions like, "Is he just going to live off his in-laws?" I let those comments go, but they did bother me just a bit. One day while mowing the fields, I had the thought that perhaps I could be successful on my own and make some money to help the camp. I decided to go work for my own family's business—the one thing that I thought I would never do. I decided then that I would team up with my father to make our business an even bigger success and also share Jesus. In the back of my mind, I was also thinking I would prove any naysayer wrong who thought I could not achieve success on my own.

About ten years later, *Duck Dynasty* became quite the phenomenon. I think we still hold the record for the most-watched non-scripted show in cable history. Our season three finale had 9.6 million viewers and our season four opener had 11.8 million viewers.[1] *Crazy.* As I mentioned earlier, the company Dad started in 1972, Duck Commander, has now been selling duck calls for over fifty years. Year forty was when the show came out, and our lives changed forever.

I was not only on the show but was also what they call an executive producer. That basically means I had to be in every meeting that pertained to the production. Along with that, for many years, I had been the CEO of Duck Commander. That means I managed the company that had already been doing well before the show started, but after being on TV, we became more successful than ever.

Hey, I get it. No one wants to hear some guy who's had success crying over his first-world problems, right? But here's the truth of the matter: the whole *Duck Dynasty* experience nearly killed my soul. Not the show necessarily, but everything that came with it. I was pulled in every direction every day. I quickly found out there's no playbook for skyrocketing success.

With our newfound fame, it seemed that everyone wanted a piece of us. Business opportunities, sponsorships, speaking engagements, and plenty of advice on how we should handle this success came flooding in. I was worried not only about my job, career, and family at that point but also my parents, brothers, and their families as well. I felt the weight of all their success on my shoulders. "Heavy is the head that wears the crown," they say. The real problem was that I started to forget the One who *really* wears the crown.

Don't get me wrong; the show did so much good, and still does. It was amazing. I believe it was from God. But just like that ol' muddy creek, there were underwater stumps everywhere. Thing is, you don't always hit stumps head-on. Sometimes the boat just glides over and you feel it. You tell your buddy, "That was close. That could have been really bad." As I was flying through life, I could feel those stumps as they tilted my boat, all the while hearing a voice whispering, "You better slow down."

Before long, I was looking more and more like those foolish boaters in Cypress Creek I used to laugh at who didn't know any better. Here I was, just like those guys with the big engines I used to see as a kid. The problem started innocently enough with a curious turn off the river into a new creek I had never navigated before. Then it happened . . . a broke propeller.

During our five-year heyday with the show, I was hanging out with a bunch of rock stars—everyone from celebrities to presidents to billionaires to megachurch pastors—but I was *not* a rock star. And then there were the tens of thousands of fans we met at the countless events where we appeared. Life was running very hot and very fast. It was all quite intoxicating, so I thought actual intoxication might help. Because we all secretly want to be rock stars, right? A shift of priority here. A neglect of my faith there. A boundary crossed. By now, my boat was drifting.

My first priority—faith—was still there, but rather than look like a blazing fire as it had been all my life, it became more like a bed of coals with some ash on top. Still very warm down deep, but without some new wood, it was on the verge of becoming cold. By the end of those five years, I would often think back to when my fire was blazing hot.

With family as our second pillar, my marriage was not in a good place—because *I* wasn't in a good place. Work and success had seemingly slid up to the top of the priority list. It wasn't like I woke up one morning and shouted, "I am now going to make my job and the pursuit of money my number one goal!" But that's exactly where I ended up.

When my marriage propeller got obliterated, it wasn't just *my* motor but my wife's as well. Because we are in the same boat. By that point, it wasn't like I just hit the stump—I was thrown out into the water. So Korie and I treated this like a 911 emergency. We interrupted life and found help. Counseling was so important to begin to patch up a bunch of mistakes. The road was long and hard. The way was dark, but the thing about letting in light is that even a tiny bit can be spotted in the night and can help you navigate your way through.

Hitting rock bottom is never fun. It was a lonely time. I didn't share my feelings, even with my closest friends. Mostly I just talked to God and listened to worship music nonstop. I grabbed hold of the lyrics to those songs like I was hanging on to a small tree in the rising floodwaters of the creek. I knew I couldn't survive like this, but at least it kept me from sinking. The words seemed to minister to me in my brokenness. To this day, when I'm in a worship service, I often cry the entire time. If you ever see me on a plane and I'm crying, no one died; I'm just listening to worship music.

As painful as all of this is to write about, I believe it's important for me to let you know I have certainly done things in my life to disqualify me from having a conversation with anyone about God or anything of faith. Maybe you've felt like that in your life at some point. Maybe that's where you're at right now. You've written yourself off because of something in your life that you've decided disqualifies you. We listen to plenty of lies about why we aren't worthy of the Good News and why we can't share it with others.

However, the very message that I'm writing about is the Good News of Jesus. It's good because it's not based on what we've done but on what He's done for us. If it were based on our own goodness, none of us would qualify. The Good News is that Jesus heals the pain, shines His light into the darkness, covers sin and shame, and makes life glorious again. No matter how cold we feel our faith becomes, God is always ready and willing to breathe life back into the flame.

I remember one interviewer asking me, "Who *is* Willie

Robertson?" I thought about that question for weeks. Because, at the time, I wasn't really sure. I knew who I was *supposed* to be and who I *wanted* to be. But I didn't think my life looked like either of those. It doesn't matter how big and cool and powerful the boat is when your propeller breaks.

But my story is really no different than yours, is it? The particulars might not be the same, but without a Savior, we are all lost, all stuck in waters without a way to get back home on our own.

> Though I have fallen, I will rise. Though I sit in darkness, the LORD will be my light. . . . He will bring me out into the light; I will see his righteousness. (Micah 7:8–9)

A ROOKIE GOSPELER

Through those hard days, I thought a lot about how things were back when I was a kid, when my fire for God was burning brighter. The earliest "Bible study" I remember leading was around seventh grade. I was on a school bus sitting by a kid named Brian. I had my Bible in hand and went after him pretty hard. When he couldn't answer the questions I was asking about his faith, I pounced. I remember him in tears. My heart was in the right place, but my approach was very unrefined and misguided.

Throughout my school years, I learned more and more each time I shared the Gospel, and I went on to have hundreds of sit-down talks with other kids. Believe it or not, most of them were eager to have a conversation about faith. I would read them Bible verses or recite the ones I had committed to memory. I learned most of this from listening to my father do the same with so many who ended up at our house down by the river.

I remember Sean, a boy I baptized early on in my high school days. He always made me smile whenever he mentioned his "babbitism." There was a foreign exchange student from Germany who was the first person to boldly profess to me that he had no belief in God. He didn't even think God was real! Not sure what to say next, I wondered, *Well, what do you tell a person like that?*

Bottom line: I was all in on sharing Jesus. I wasn't a perfect teen, for sure, but I loved hearing people's stories of where they were in their faith journey. And when they would respond with questions I couldn't answer, I would circle back to Dad to get his take on how I could best help them. As I had more and more conversations about Jesus, I knew it was important for me to be a disciple, a student of the Gospel.

MY FAVORITE FISHERMAN

As a young kid who grew up on a river in a family that was in the fishing business, I fell in love with Jesus, who incidentally had a lot of friends who were fishermen. I was always pretty bold about sharing Him with whoever would listen. I think that's why I've always loved reading about Peter in the Gospels, because he was also a fisherman who followed Jesus. In fact, a giant haul of fish would be the turning point where he decided to dedicate his life to this man who proclaimed to be the Son of God.

As a child, one thing I understood very well was the thrill of a huge catch. I had seen that happen many times in our nets on the river. I knew the struggle to get them into the boat. So when Jesus called the shot that Simon Peter would bring in an enormous load of fish, I could see that moment very clearly in my mind. Peter decided he was in. And so was I.

When Jesus told Simon Peter He would teach him to be a "fisher of men," I understood that as well. Even being so young, I was consumed with trying to gather people into the kingdom of God, just like pulling a huge haul into our boat. I knew it took work: the Scriptures have to be studied; you have to care about people; it takes time and patience. There are lots of failed attempts, but when someone embraces the Good News, there is nothing as satisfying. Much like fishing.

Like the interviewer asked me, I'd like to ask Peter the same question: "Who is Simon Peter?" The rock who built the church? Or the disciple who denied even knowing Jesus?

Luke chapter 5 tells us the story of how it all started:

One day as Jesus was standing by the Lake of Gennesaret, the people were crowding around him and listening to the word of God. He saw at the water's edge two boats, left there by the fishermen, who were washing their nets. He got into one of the boats, the one belonging to Simon, and asked him to put out a little from shore. Then he sat down and taught the people from the boat. When he had finished speaking, he said to Simon, "Put out into deep water, and let down the nets for a catch." Simon answered, "Master, we've worked hard all night and haven't caught anything. But because you say so, I will let down the nets." When they had done so, they caught such a large number of fish that their nets began to break. So they signaled their partners in the other boat to come and help them, and they came and filled both boats so full that they began to sink. When Simon Peter saw this, he fell at Jesus' knees and said, "Go away from me, Lord; I am a sinful man!" For he and all his companions were astonished at the catch of fish they had taken, and so were James and John, the sons of Zebedee, Simon's partners. (Luke 5:1–10)

Peter was not formally trained. He had never been a public speaker, pursued seminary training, or earned a counseling degree. He just knew how to catch fish. *Voila!* Jesus could work with that. But Jesus didn't go out and just get a bunch of fishermen. He gathered all sorts of regular ol' folks. Not the most religious, mostly just people like you and me.

But Jesus didn't leave Peter where he was at; Jesus told Peter who he would become. After Peter boldly declared Jesus to be the long-awaited Messiah, the Son of the living God, Jesus lovingly looked him in the eyes and responded, "Blessed are you, Simon son of Jonah, for this was not revealed to you by flesh and blood, but by my Father in heaven. And I tell you that you are Peter, and on this rock I will build my church, and the gates of Hades will not overcome it" (Matthew 16:17–18).

Now, let's fast-forward to the night of Jesus' trials. Simon Peter found himself on the hot seat as Jesus was about to be put to death for His claims. Outside the place where Jesus was questioned, Peter was accused of being with Him. Not only did Peter not admit to being a follower of Jesus, he denied even knowing Him—not once, but three times! There was not a playbook for him either. Peter flat-out blew it at the most critical moment.

Now Peter was sitting out in the courtyard, and a servant girl came to him. "You also were with Jesus of Galilee," she said. But he denied it before them all. "I don't know what you're talking about," he said. Then he went out to the gateway, where another servant girl saw him and said to the people there, "This fellow was with Jesus of Nazareth." He denied it again, with an oath: "I don't know the man!" After a little while, those standing there went up to Peter and said, "Surely you are one of them; your accent gives you away." Then he began to call down curses, and he swore to them, "I don't know the man!" Immediately a rooster crowed. Then Peter remembered the word Jesus had spoken: "Before the rooster crows, you will disown me three times." And he went outside and wept bitterly. (Matthew 26:69–75)

Peter hit a huge, hidden stump head-on. His propeller was shattered. But isn't this the same kind of moment we all find ourselves in at times? We feel like life is cruising along great, and then in a moment, *bam!* We can't figure out how we got so off track. Something we swore we would never do, we just did. We promised we'd always take a stand for Jesus, but we found ourselves silent when it mattered the most. If Peter's story had ended here, it would be very sad—not just for him but for all the many lives he would one day touch.

After Jesus' crucifixion, between His resurrection and return to heaven, Peter, without a propeller, landed right back on his boat, literally. He was back on the water, right where Jesus found him in the first place. But then something happened that Peter did not see coming.

Early in the morning, Jesus stood on the shore, but the disciples did not realize that it was Jesus. He called out to them, "Friends, haven't you any fish?" "No," they answered. He said, "Throw your net on the right side of the boat and you will find some." When they did, they were unable to haul the net in because of the large number of fish. Then the disciple whom Jesus loved said to Peter, "It is the Lord!" As soon as Simon Peter heard him say, "It is the Lord," he wrapped his outer garment around him (for he had taken it off) and jumped into the water. (John 21:4–7)

The fact that Peter had gone back to fishing tells me that he was seemingly going to put his whole experience with Jesus in his pocket and lie low the rest of his days. When our TV show ended in 2017 after eleven seasons, I certainly felt the same way. I thought, *Let's get out of the spotlight and just imagine what could have been. Satan wins. I'll be quiet now. We don't have to get canceled, because we cancel ourselves!* I'm guessing Peter felt the same in this moment. That is, until Jesus showed up on the shore.

LIFE ON MISSION

Jesus' last recorded conversation with Peter was pivotal to Peter's future.

When they had finished eating, Jesus said to Simon Peter, "Simon son of John, do you love me more than these?" "Yes, Lord," he said, "you know that I love you." Jesus said, "Feed my lambs." Again Jesus said, "Simon son of John, do you love me?" He answered, "Yes, Lord, you know that I love you." Jesus said, "Take care of my sheep." The third time he said to him, "Simon son of John, do you love me?" Peter was hurt because Jesus asked him the third time, "Do you love me?" He said, "Lord, you know all things; you know that I love you." Jesus said, "Feed my sheep." (John 21:15–17)

Jesus basically said to Peter, "This is not about you, but Me, and others." Jesus stayed on His mission and completed it. As difficult as it was, He did not give up. He died not for Himself but for others. From that moment with Jesus on the beach, Peter got out of his drifting boat of shame and regret and became one of the greatest Gospelers the world has ever known. He told everyone who would listen about the Good News, right up to his own death, which is believed to be like Jesus': crucified, except upside down, to pay reverence to His Lord.

Now, can you imagine Peter's life if that final conversation hadn't happened? Jesus had to blast through the darkness Peter was feeling with a big ol' Jesus-beam of light. A simple question repeated three times, the same number of times Peter denied Him. "Peter, do you love Me?" When the answer was "Yes," Jesus gave him a mission. Mission makes regret melt away. Mission is forward. Mission is future. Regret is in the past, and Jesus obliterated the past. Time to get on mission!

This brings up the next reason I can relate to Peter so much—the way he went on to boldly proclaim his faith in the Gospel. Just a simple fisherman who had been touched by Jesus, Peter had a pivotal moment in his life that could have taken him in a whole different direction. Yet he didn't let his mistakes hold him back from telling everyone how wonderful it is to live with Jesus. By the time we start the book of Acts, we see that Peter didn't cancel himself, and other believers did not cancel him either.

The very nature of Christ's love and sacrifice covers the missteps we all have. The Jesus who paid for all that shame with His death on a cross is all we need. But oftentimes, when His grace should bolster our confidence in speaking up, our mistakes cause us to clam up and keep silent about our faith.

Peter did not try to redact the lies he told about his connection to Jesus even though they had produced his greatest regret. It was all part of his journey that I'm sure fueled him to be even bolder. I'm thankful we have stories like that in the Bible so we can gain strength and confidence when we want to give up or quit. Paul reflected on this in his second letter to the Corinthians: "My grace is sufficient for you, for my power is made perfect in weakness" (12:9). It's not the story we should tell *despite* our shortcomings; it's the story we tell *because* we do fall short, the reason we all need the Good News.

> IT'S NOT THE STORY WE SHOULD TELL *DESPITE* OUR SHORTCOMINGS; IT'S THE STORY WE TELL *BECAUSE* WE DO FALL SHORT, THE REASON WE ALL NEED THE GOOD NEWS.

In Acts chapter 1, after Jesus left His disciples to go up to heaven, who was there, organizing the young church to get ready to explode on the world? Peter. When the Holy Spirit showed up in the physical absence of Jesus, who was there, leading the disciples? Peter. In Acts chapter 2, who got up right in the middle of a dangerous religious climate that had just put Jesus to death, where a lot of people knew he had denied even knowing the man three times, and spoke to the crowd of thousands? Yes, Peter.

So, what happened to this guy?

How do you go from walking away from the Lord to running right into the jaws of peril for Him?

After Jesus gave him his mission, Peter decided his life was going to look radically different. He knew that everything Jesus said was going to take place. Knowing now that he and Jesus were good, Peter went out to tell others so they could also be right with Jesus. In fact, he knew that to *not* share with people would be incredibly selfish.

Peter had just walked around for the past three years with the Personification of unselfishness—Jesus Christ Himself. Think about what Jesus represented. A Man who gave of Himself to everyone. A Man who gave up His own life. A Man who used some of His last days on earth, after He came back from the dead and was headed to heaven, to take the time to have a pep talk with Peter.

Peter knew he had to tell others. That was his Jesus-driven mission. He realized that, in the grand scheme of life, fish didn't matter, boats didn't matter, nets didn't matter, and yes, even his own life was not that big of a deal. Now his voice mattered. The Gospel mattered. Because Jesus changed his whole life and eternity, he would now live his life like Jesus had on this earth.

ON-THE-JOB TRAINING

My hope is that, like Peter and me, you won't think about the past but instead think about what could happen in your future. Many of us find ourselves in that same boat: we often give all sorts of reasons why we have disqualified ourselves from sharing our faith. We need to break down all those lies and myths and tools of the Evil One that keep too many of us quiet about our story, about Jesus' story.

I get that some of you reading this might not have a clue how to share your faith, how to help lead a person to the Lord. You don't feel "qualified." You don't know the Bible like you feel you should. Or you may believe your life is such a mess that you're the last person who should try to help others. Maybe no one ever told you that telling others about Jesus was part of the deal. So you hope that someone out there tells others—but it certainly ain't you! Well, I want to challenge you to rethink that.

Here's an important question: What if it's not only *part* of the deal but the *whole* deal? What if living a life on mission to share your faith is the very thing that helps to keep your faith at the top of your priority list? What if in your top three things in life, faith came first? What might your life look like if you woke up every morning and the first thing you said was, "How can I share the love and light I get from Jesus with someone else today?"

I want to rewind to something profound Jesus said when He first met Peter, way back at the beginning:

> Jesus, walking by the Sea of Galilee, saw two brothers, Simon called Peter, and Andrew his brother, casting a net into the sea; for they were fishermen. Then He said to them, "Follow Me, and I will make you fishers of men." (Matthew 4:18–19 NKJV)

"I will make you fishers of men." Jesus used the analogy of their career to set a foundation with Peter and the others. He let them know what the priority would be. He did something for them by giving them a huge catch, but then let them know, "From here on, it's not going to be about you, but others."

Jesus' phrase "I will make you," sounds like He's going to do some training. These men didn't just have that ability naturally. They had to grow in it. Sadly, I think it's all too rare that people come to the Lord and then hear, "Great, now let's go get some more people!" We might hear, "Now try to go to church" or "Give some money." These are fine things, but if someone we know is lost in their sin, their family is falling apart, or they are on the verge of suicide, and we tell them, "Hey, it's okay. I can help because I go to church," that's not really going to offer much.

Here's the point—I feel like we have gotten away from some key foundational practices that Jesus wanted His church to do. Specifically, He asked them to tell others about Him. Jesus let Peter know right from the start that He was going after people. And Jesus' last instructions were about the same thing: "Go and make disciples" (Matthew 28:19). Be Gospelers.

Maybe we signed up for Jesus with a raised hand in a church building and assumed our life's journey as a believer meant constantly working on ourselves, listening to others' beliefs and opinions of the Bible, and hopefully being blessed in this life with money and safety as we raise our families. We don't talk to anyone about Jesus, because when we raised our hand, no one mentioned that.

That's why many of us have no idea how to share the Gospel. We aren't trained or taught. If I'm being real, we may never even think about it, or just when we might begin to get the courage to actually say something, we remember that our propeller is broken. We've hit some stumps and have been floating in the water. Maybe for some time. Maybe a long time.

When your boat does not have an operational propeller, you are unable to take people where they need to go. "Hop in my boat, and we'll just float around." Who wants to do that? So naturally we don't ask people to get into the boat. It's as though we see desperate people all along the shore who need a lift, and rather than yelling, "Where do you need to go?" we whisper, "My propeller's broken . . . sorry."

Jesus got into Simon Peter's boat when there was not a lot of hope. Catching no fish, Peter was tired, with little future, meaning, and purpose. Broke. Drifting. He desperately needed to see something positive and dynamic. Jesus showed the disciples just what they needed, to the point where they said to each other, "Okay, He's got our attention." If they had been at a church today, I guess their heads would be bowed, eyes closed, and hands raised.

But don't miss what happened next. This could be the key to unlocking your true meaning and purpose as you follow Jesus. He offered to train them to do a job. He took a risk and had a conversation. He let them know that, first, He cared about them. He let them know He had God's power. And then He said, "Let's get to work."

Maybe we get off track because it was drilled into our heads that it's not our works that save us, but the grace of Jesus. That is very true. There is *nothing* you can do to earn your way to heaven. So when we think about following Jesus and hear that He has a job for us, we think of "work," which sounds like "works," and that makes us nervous. Yes, it is a gift—but we are not meant to take our gift, unwrap it, put it on our shelf, and then just stare at it and smile. We're meant to use it!

GET BACK OUT ON THE WATER

I have a big boat that's sheltered under a dock I built for it. As I write this, the boat has a cover on it. The boat is supported by a system that keeps it out of the water when it's not being used. Because it's elevated, you can see the big propeller that moves it. It's not in the water, so I know that unless something like a tornado hits, that boat is safe and sound.

Sadly, my boat stays like that way too much. I say sadly because my boat wasn't designed and built to be protected and kept out of the water. It is meant to be *on* the water, *in* the water, full of people. When I go fast, my boat can pull folks hanging onto ropes and make a wake for someone to surf on. When I go slow, you can see fish below the surface of the water and relax to the music played on its sound system. But *every time* my boat is in the water, there is always a chance that the propeller can hit something.

When I went to look at this boat, the guy sold me on all the features. He knew all about it and that I would love it. But he didn't mention my schedule. He didn't say, "Hey, if you don't make time to enjoy this and actually be on the water, this may not be for you." And he also didn't bring up broken propellers. He assumed I wouldn't put a bunch of money into a boat and then keep it out of the water, away from its purpose.

Even in my darkest times, the one thing that never left me was my desire to share my faith. Even the days when I was not at my best, I always managed to talk about what I knew lived in me and gave me hope. In fact, oftentimes, the very nature of telling others about Jesus would get me back in line. When you

> **WHEN YOU TELL PEOPLE ABOUT THE LIGHT, IT'S MORE DIFFICULT TO LIVE IN DARKNESS.**

tell people about the Light, it's more difficult to live in darkness.

Just one conversation led Peter to jump out of his boat and leave his entire life behind again, even though there would be many propeller repairs along the way. In Jesus' last conversation with Peter, He let him know that his spiritual propeller was as good as new. This wasn't just a high-five moment of "We did it! It's over, so now go find a little piece of property by the Sea of Galilee, make babies, find a church, get in a small group, and do a little good while you're here on earth." The message was, "Get back out there!"

There was another time in my life when I could relate to Peter. After *Duck Dynasty* was over, I decided to lie low and avoid people. You know, just float and avoid the stumps. Go back to where I started. Back to what I knew best. For me, that was Camp Ch-Yo-Ca, a place I associate with a time in my life when I was unknown by people. From time to time, I would still go out there to help with projects. So, there I was, deep in the woods with a burn pile of limbs and my dog. I had my worship music going and was confident this was where I would spend all my extra time for the rest of my life.

Suddenly, from somewhere in the middle of the woods, I heard a young guy yell my name. As I looked up and saw him walking toward me, I wondered, *How did this guy find me?* I figured it was a fan of the show and someone had told him I was out here, but that was not the case. "You remember me?" he asked.

"Not really," I responded.

"You baptized me years ago right here on this property when

I was a teenager!" he said with a huge smile. And then it all came back to me. Not just his story, which I remembered well, but all of it came back to me—stories from my past that were not regrets but victories. It was as if Jesus Himself had sent this man out here to say, "Willie, we're good! I made you good with the Gospel!"

From that moment, Jesus started reminding me of my purpose, my mission. He began to help me line up the family motto back into the right priorities. He let me know that, because of Him, my propeller was good as new. I realized that, in the grand scheme of life, fame didn't matter, TV shows didn't matter, duck calls didn't matter, and yes, even my own life was not that big of a deal. But my voice mattered. The Gospel mattered. So, just like my favorite fisherman, I knew I had to get back out there and tell others. I must tell others. That is my Jesus-driven mission.

Because I am a Gospeler.

Part 2

THE GOSPEL STORY

Four

STORYTELLER

SHE STUCK HER HEAD IN THE DOOR AND SHOUTED, "WHAT IS *THIS?*"
Even though there's a small sign above the door that says
First Step, I think she was curious what this little room was, just
outside the auditorium of the church. I was in there reading over
my notes, waiting for anyone who might come in to talk about
Jesus after the service concluded. But the pastor was just getting
started with his sermon when she peeked in. This was a rare time
when someone dropped by *during* church and didn't wait until
afterward.

"This is the place you can take the first step toward Jesus
Christ," I responded.

"Oh s***!" she said rather loudly as the pastor was preaching
just a few feet away.

Another one of the pastors, who was standing beside me,
suddenly looked frozen with fear, then said, "Okay, Willie, I'll let
you get to it." And he rushed out of the room.

As I laughed, I said to the young woman, "Come on in, you may need to hear this."

We had set up this room specifically for people who had spiritual questions so we could try to reach them better. We felt that many people who come to a church service may not get their questions answered in a personal way—especially folks who may have never taken that first step toward Jesus.

Alyssa let me know right away that, in her thirty years, this was the first time she had set foot in a church building. After the singing, she quickly got bored, so she just wandered off into this very room where I was ready to share the Gospel. I asked her to share her story with me, and, boy, did she ever have a story! As she talked, she showed me some kind of New Age crystals and cards she carried around with her and shared about her troubled past. Alyssa had come simply because a neighbor had invited her to visit.

When she was done, I started writing Bible passages on the white board and drawing out the aspects of the Gospel. I like to begin with a horizontal line right across the middle. Using Scripture, I helped her discover the difference in a life defined by sin and one set free by the Gospel, and how she could cross the line of faith herself. At some point, Alyssa asked if she could draw on the board as well. I said, "Sure," and handed her some markers. She then started doodling as we talked about her life. She didn't know much about the Lord, but at least she was there, and I gave her the Gospel in the simplest form.

About the time I was finished, church let out. Eventually, her neighbors peeked into the room and exclaimed, "Alyssa! There you are!" They had no clue where she had wandered off to.

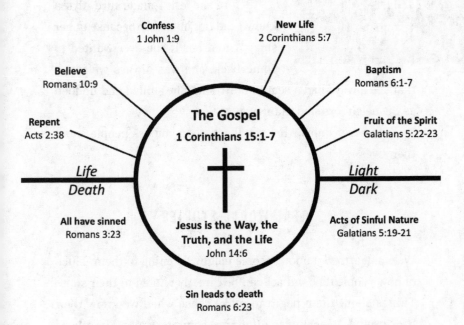

This is what I like to draw out when sharing the Gospel.

> YOU NEVER KNOW WHAT YOU'LL GET WHEN YOU ASK PEOPLE ABOUT THEIR LIVES.

After I smiled and shared that we had a great talk, she told them, "This guy is a teacher and he told me about Jesus, the Holy Spirit, and . . . uh, one more, but I can't remember the last one."

Before she left, I made sure Alyssa knew I did not judge her because of her story. I told her if she ever wanted to come back, she was always welcome, that she always had a seat in our room. She smiled and nodded as the neighbors said thank you.

You never know what you'll get when you ask people about their lives.

REAL-WORLD STORIES

We can learn a lot about people just by listening to them. Much of how people talk and act can be directly related to their story. Things about them begin to make sense when we know their background. We can also often find common ground in others' experiences that connect with our own. If you ever want to tell someone a thing or two, it helps to begin by just listening.

One of the first steps for a Gospeler is gathering the person's spiritual story. *Do you have a faith? If so, when and where did your faith start? How is it going now? Are there any issues? Do you have any questions about life?* Gospelers gather stories with a purpose in mind. The mission is to learn in order to understand someone so you can show you care about them, and *then* have a conversation that could lead to a whole new story!

I would hate to just gather information without offering hope. We need to listen but not *just* listen. Hearing questions, doubts, or any damage the person has suffered without offering solutions would be really sad. Can you imagine if someone told you he or she was in pain and not automatically asking if the person had seen a doctor? Even worse would be if you'd had that same pain, went to a doctor and were cured, and didn't offer your own path to victory over the pain.

Speaking of real-world stories, my favorite TV shows are *Dateline*, *My 600-lb Life*, and *Dr. Phil*—all shows, by the way, I would never want to be on! Oftentimes, there's a big problem, and then a solution is found (hopefully). They most often show extreme situations, which is why it makes for great TV. We connect to the stories because, being flawed humans, we can all relate on some level.

"True crime" shows fascinate me because these situations really happen, every day. Awful stories. I am always floored by what makes people do certain things. They usually follow a similar storyline of lust, greed, affairs, envy, or revenge, with sin always at the root. And often in these stories, the worst happens. Someone gets murdered. A line gets crossed. Then the police come and lay out their own line around the entire area with yellow crime-scene tape.

Most episodes have a "look back" section showing home videos of the person as a child when life seemed better or more normal, long before everything spiraled down a dark path. Trouble starts. Something terrible happens. There may be a recorded 911 call. Then the questions come: What really happened? Why? How? This is where the plot twists come in. Lies are exposed. DNA is discovered. Cell phones are tracked. Someone has broken the law, and there are consequences. Investigators are trying to find out the *true* story of what happened.

My 600-lb Life is a show where the person can't say, "I don't have a problem," because it's very obvious. Often, pain and damage from the past are at the heart of the weight gain. The person has been hurt and is now killing themself with food. As the stories are told, you can almost always see when life started going off the rails. Hearing their stories causes any initial judgment to soon be replaced with compassion.

There are usually enablers involved in these situations. The person is literally trapped in the problems and, often, in their own house. We root for them as they try to find a new way to live. Before weight-loss surgery can take place, a commitment has to be made, because the removal of fat is not the end of the story; it's just the beginning. There must be real-life change or it just comes back.

Then there's *Dr. Phil*. This show is the one I can identify with most. I have certainly had issues that could have put me in his chair, especially back when my propeller was broken! It all starts with problems that first have to be identified. The whole time, Dr. Phil is trying to find the real story. Once the root issue is discovered, a plan is crafted to deal with and get rid of it. At the start of the show, there seems to be no hope, but then breakthroughs begin.

With all three programs, there is a recurring theme: get to the *real* story. *Dateline* and other true crime shows almost always have two different paths—one true, one false. *Dr. Phil* has to get to the real story as well, all while dealing with feelings and personalities. Even *My 600-lb Life* has people searching for the real story behind how and why folks have gotten themselves into their predicament.

There's another aspect all those shows have in common: at the beginning, the producer, director, and, likely, the host already know the ending. But they never start there to tell the story. They first present the viewer with a conflict. That's my approach too. I don't jump to provide an answer and tell someone the Gospel without finding out about the person's life, leading up to the moment we're talking to each other. There's usually some kind of conflict to discover first. When I'm initially getting into a conversation with folks, I may not even lead with Jesus. Like those TV shows, people need to identify the problems in their own lives before they will go on the hunt for the solution. Also, if they have any preconceived notions about Jesus, or have no idea who He is or what He did for them, He may not matter to them in any way, at least not at first. Even though everyone's story is different, Jesus has a solution for *every* problem.

> EVEN THOUGH EVERYONE'S STORY IS DIFFERENT, JESUS HAS A SOLUTION FOR EVERY PROBLEM.

SIMPLE QUESTION, ETERNAL ANSWER

In John chapter 4, there is an incredible passage where Jesus listened to a woman's story and it led to a complete life change. By the end of the conversation, she was completely different because

IT ALL STARTED WITH A CONVERSATION SPARKED BY ONE SIMPLE QUESTION.

He came into her story. And boy, did she ever have a story to tell! Before *and* after Jesus! In fact, afterward, she went to her whole town to tell of how He changed her life—even though before, like many people I talk with, she had no clue who Jesus even was.

It all started with a conversation sparked by one simple question.

Oftentimes, when we think of telling people about Jesus, our minds convince us it is super invasive and difficult, when in reality it can begin just like this:

> When a Samaritan woman came to draw water, Jesus said to her, "Will you give me a drink?" (v. 7)

Jesus was thirsty and asked for a drink of water. That was it. Who would ever think that there would be many lives changed forever just by asking, "Hey, can I get a drink of water?" But that's how easily it can happen. That's the power of Jesus. If you have ever gotten thirsty and asked for a drink, you can be a Gospeler.

When Jesus asked her that question, He was opening up a conversation to hear her story—and to tell her His story. In the culture of the day, because she was a woman, a Samaritan, and a person with a questionable reputation, just by speaking to her, He showed her that He cared about her life. Think about it: if you really don't care, why would you ask anything about anyone's life? In most places these days, folks walk right by each other all the time and rarely speak because most are caught up in their own worlds. We have our own problems, so we think the last thing we need is to get involved in someone else's.

Jesus decided to get involved and quickly steered the conversation to His mission:

> The Samaritan woman said to him, "You are a Jew and I am a Samaritan woman. How can you ask me for a drink?" (For Jews do not associate with Samaritans.) Jesus answered her, "If you knew the gift of God and who it is that asks you for a drink, you would have asked him and he would have given you living water." "Sir," the woman said, "you have nothing to draw with and the well is deep. Where can you get this living water? Are you greater than our father Jacob, who gave us the well and drank from it himself, as did also his sons and his livestock?"
>
> Jesus answered, "Everyone who drinks this water will be thirsty again, but whoever drinks the water I give them will never thirst. Indeed, the water I give them will become in them a spring of water welling up to eternal life." (John 4:9–14)

The easy path for Jesus would have been to follow social norms and never ask a question. He seemed to be opening up a can of worms. But Jesus didn't think like we do. He didn't just look for an opportunity; He *made* an opportunity. He went there on purpose with a purpose.

Jesus started talking about eternal life, Living Water. These things sounded amazing, but she had no idea what He was saying. He was offering gifts—Living Water and eternal life—and she was concerned with buckets, ladles, and earthly ancestors.

When gathering someone's story, don't be surprised when

> I NEVER EXPECT
> PEOPLE WHO DON'T
> KNOW JESUS TO
> ACT LIKE PEOPLE
> WHO DO.

they have no clue what Jesus is all about. I never expect people who don't know Jesus to act like people who do—like when Alyssa blurted out the curse word at church. That's just where she was coming from. And like this woman at the well, Alyssa was willing to listen, which is where conversations start.

When most folks can't see or feel something "real," they tend to get disinterested. They ask questions like, "Can it help with my bills?" or "Can it make my kids behave?" This is the introduction to faith and the beginning of moving beyond what we can see or feel at the moment to believing in something we cannot see. Jesus was starting to introduce these ideas to this woman.

Jesus then dropped the earthly for the spiritual. At this point, the woman was either going to ask more questions or just walk away.

He asked for a drink of earthly water to start the conversation and then gave her His story about water that springs into His gift of eternal life. Notice how He stayed on the path of the topic they started on. Just a conversation that kept leading more and more toward what was eternal and what Jesus could bring to her life. But here's another really important point: Jesus didn't say the same thing to every person He encountered. This was another tailor-made conversation just for this woman that led to the same conclusion as all His stories—to think about heaven, not earth, and to please God, not people.

When we talk to others about spiritual things or Jesus specifically, we may feel we have to say exactly the right things. We can become sort of robotic and give a one-size-fits-all message, but we need to just go where their story leads, always pointing to Jesus as the answer. The Good News is the same, no matter how we end up there.

At this point, the woman was starting to understand.

Sir, give me this water so that I won't get thirsty and have to keep coming here to draw water. (v. 15)

This was the crucial part of their conversation because she was now asking *for* something. She wanted to know more. This changed everything. When someone asks for help, the implication is that they are open to doing whatever is necessary to receive what is offered. There was also an indication that her life was not where it needed to be. This is a best-case scenario when sharing the Gospel with someone. They ask, so it's not being forced. It's not our job to push the Good News down anyone's throat. In fact, Jesus never forced Himself on anyone. He always offered a choice.

Back to my favorite TV shows. *My 600-lb Life* always gets to this same place. The choice is always the big moment. The person states that they want to make a change. Believe me, Dr. Now, the doctor on the show, will make sure they are 100 percent serious. If they are not truly ready, he will just send them away. Because, obviously, it takes true commitment to lose hundreds of pounds.

When the woman asked for the Living Water, she didn't truly even understand what it was or who was talking to her at the time. The somewhat awkward conversation led up to the moment when Jesus went deeper. Not in the well of water, but the well of her life. Before long, the original request for a drink of water seemed like a distant memory.

GETTING REAL

So why was this woman interested in the Living Water? Because she had a need. That's when Jesus took the conversation further and asked her to invite her husband.

> He told her, "Go, call your husband and come back."
> "I have no husband," she replied. (vv. 16–17)

Jesus could have said, "Great, then let's move on." But instead, He went on to talk about her complicated relationship roller coaster.

> "You have had five husbands, and the man you now have is not your husband. What you have just said is quite true." (v. 18)

We need to be clear that Jesus had no interest in embarrassing this woman. In fact, He literally went out of His way to help her. This is where I see the biggest difference in what Jesus did and what we often do today in our churches and conversations. At this point, if someone asks about Jesus, we may pray with them and tell them they've got Jesus in their lives now. Done and done! However, we too often don't go to the next level of hearing more about their story. Jesus knew exactly what her story was but still wanted to hear all of it. He wanted her to get it out and deal with it. Because the entire time, He had her best interests at heart.

Jesus knew that even though He told her she could have living water, she was still going to have to go back to the town where everyone knew about her life. She may have changed, but the people hadn't. Perhaps, because of her past, she may decide to just keep this little conversation to herself. Telling everyone that she talked to a strange man might just make her sound like she was up to her old tricks. But Jesus pressed even further. He wanted her story. He wanted all the details. Nothing she shared would repel Him, as perhaps it did with many she knew.

> THE TRUTH IS, ALL OUR STORIES ARE FULL OF BAGGAGE. WE ALL HAVE ISSUES, AND WE ALL HAVE A PAST.

The truth is, all our stories are full of baggage. We all have issues, and we all have a past. Even today, when we seek help with problems, whether in an environment that's clinical, church-related, tied to a self-help organization, or just a small group, we look at where we have been and want to be better. God-centered program or not, most of these have the same thing in common—you have to deal with your past. Jesus wrote the playbook for redemption, so He knew that He had to first help this woman deal with her past so she could walk into her future.

She was telling the truth, which was very important. But she was not willing to go all the way and tell Him everything. That makes sense because she'd just met Him. She could have lied, but she didn't. He was telling her that He already knew and was still there. He still cared enough to talk to her. Jesus wanted her to see that He was a safe person who wanted her to never be stuck where she had been. He was the Living Water that would revolutionize her life.

Jesus patiently drawing out the truth and listening to her response reminds me of *Dateline* when folks are asked about what happened. Interviewers or police are trying to get the real story. Many times they respond with slivers of truth, or sometimes outright lies. Sometimes the investigators already know the answers, but they still ask the questions to see how the person will respond or even if they will confess to the crime. Jesus is like the investigator who's asking questions but already knows the answers. Then, when you give your life to Him, He becomes your Defense Attorney as well. How? Because God is the Judge. If you were on trial and the judge's son was your defense attorney, you would feel pretty good about your chances!

Our screwed-up stories with all their baggage are exactly why Jesus came to earth, to make those stories new and different. Jesus listened and offered solutions. This is an important step for us to take as well. Listen, but offer hope. I know lots of people who listen to others' issues but have a hard time pointing toward any answers. We get shy about dealing with some of the chaos we hear. Jesus took it head-on and got that out of the way first. Just like this woman, the worse your past, the more powerful the testimony. That's exactly what's coming for her.

Our story can be told by us or by others, or at least their version of it. I'm sure Jesus could have found out what others thought this woman's story was just by going into the town. The gossip about her was probably constant. Even in our big cities or small towns today, the workplace can get pretty nasty when it comes to people talking about each other. So stories about a woman with five former husbands who is currently living with a guy get around pretty fast, back then and today. (In fact, this story would probably be all over Facebook, complete with pictures!)

WITH JESUS, *EVERY* STORY CAN HAVE A NEW ENDING.

What others know of our story can also get passed around, whether we like it or not. Oftentimes, it is told by others like a bad country song: with no hope, no resolution, and no redemption. People love telling and hearing awful stories as long as they are about others. Perhaps that's because it makes their stories seem better. But with Jesus, *every* story can have a new ending. For years, people can let their pasts define them, trapped by mistakes, which then become their identity. Yet when our stories crash into Jesus' story, life change can happen.

Paul said in Romans 1:16, "For I am not ashamed of the gospel, because it is the power of God that brings salvation to everyone who believes." The Gospel has the power, not us. We just have to share it. All the work has been done. We simply tell the story.

We must realize, just like this woman was looking for something that Jesus had, people are looking for the Good News that we have. We just need to get past all the fears and distractions. When we listen to people's stories, we will hear the brokenness and emptiness, the search for something meaningful. We will pick up on the dissatisfaction with life, work, family, and a whole host of other issues. We might hear a longing for community, or a struggle with loneliness, or a slew of bad decisions that have made life unbearable. When we provide a caring ear, people will open up with their stories.

But you won't always hear brokenness or hardships. You might just see pride. You could be met with arrogance, as if they have little need for anything, let alone a Savior. They may not realize they are searching. People can feel like they have everything they need or feel that everything they have was earned by and for themselves. Some believe that they're on top of the world. Their story doesn't include Jesus, and they are totally fine with that.

But having answers for every situation is the whole point of this book. Everyone's hurting somehow. Everyone's dealing with sin or the consequences of sin in some way. And Jesus solves everyone's sin problem. There are many different ways to get the story of Jesus to others. You may choose simply to share how He has changed your story. That should come naturally because it's your story! There can be no argument against that. While listening to problems is where the conversation starts, pointing toward answers is where lives can change. The answer to what we are all looking for is found in the Gospel. Forgiveness of sin. A new life. Hope.

Jesus listened to this woman and gave her some good news. Immediately after her encounter with Him, she went and told her story to the whole town, and as a result, "many of the Samaritans from that town believed in him because of the woman's testimony" (John 4:39).

It is truly remarkable how her life started to change immediately. What began as an uncomfortable conversation led to a clear answer that ended with many others following Jesus. But it all started with one simple question: "Can I get a drink of water?"

DIFFERENT WOMAN, SAME JESUS

Let's move from John chapter 4 to chapter 8, where a woman was brought to Jesus because some men were trying to get to the bottom of her story. She had sinned like they all had. But they were going to be the judge, jury, and executioner for her, literally. Jesus jumped right in and did something very interesting.

> When they kept on questioning him, he straightened up and said to them, "Let any one of you who is without sin be the first to throw a stone at her." (v. 7)

He pretty much asked if any of them had ever sinned. Jesus was getting into their stories!

Then, He bent down and wrote something in the dirt; He might have been using some sort of visual in His explanation. It must have worked, because they all left—every last one of them—and then Jesus went back to her story, asking,

> "Woman, where are they? Has no one condemned you?"
> "No one, sir," she said.
> "Then neither do I condemn you," Jesus declared. "Go now and leave your life of sin." (vv. 10–11)

She was not only saved from a stoning but lived to tell others about Jesus.

I assure whoever I am talking to that I have no judgment after hearing their story, because I'm not the judge of the person's life. I'm only sharing with them because I care, even if I don't know them at all. Especially today, lots of people feel that no one really cares about them. The fact that someone is taking the time to listen and have a conversation can make a huge difference. I tell the person, "Hey, I don't get paid to do this. I just have something that helped me and may help you. That's all." This can go a long way with folks, just like it did for both women in those two different encounters with Jesus. He showed them He cared by helping them for no apparent reason.

With most people I meet, whether it's a onetime encounter on a plane or the beginning of a longer connection, I like to start by asking if they have a faith. I don't ask if they go to church, because if they do, they will usually include it in their story. I may ask if they think there is life after this life. What does that look like for them? I may ask if they believe there is a God or what their thoughts are on Jesus. Sometimes they may initiate the conversation with a specific question.

As the person is sharing with me, if I have anything available to write on, I like to jot down some aspects of their story—key points I can refer back to, especially at the end of a conversation. (That's why I love that Jesus was writing something in the dirt in the John 8 story.) Sometimes the story changes as we go along. Because I'm asking personal questions, people may be guarded because they have learned to be that way to survive. But again, there is no telling what can of worms we are going to open up.

I may hear they have never understood the Bible. Or they are not sure if there is a God. They might say they believe if you are "good," you will go to heaven. Sometimes, they add, "if there is a heaven." I've found that stories can be like songs. There are millions of them, and no two are the same. Maybe similar, but not the same. While songs all come from the same collection of notes, each one is slightly different. So when you have conversations, some may be drastically different from anything you've heard, while others are very similar. But the Gospel will always be the same; it's just your approach to how you share this Good News that's the variable.

TWO CHOICES, TWO LIFESTYLES

After hearing someone's story, I often go first to the book of Galatians and read where Paul wrote in chapter 5 about two different lives we can live:

> When you follow the desires of your sinful nature, the results are very clear: sexual immorality, impurity, lustful pleasures, idolatry, sorcery, hostility, quarreling, jealousy, outbursts of anger, selfish ambition, dissension, division, envy, drunkenness, wild parties, and other sins like these. Let me tell you again, as I have before, that anyone living that sort of life will not inherit the Kingdom of God.
>
> But the Holy Spirit produces this kind of fruit in our lives: love, joy, peace, patience, kindness, goodness, faithfulness, gentleness, and self-control. There is no law against these things! Those who belong to Christ Jesus have nailed the passions and desires of their sinful nature to his cross and crucified them there. (vv. 19–24 NLT)

Paul described a very clear line here of what it looks like to live for Jesus and what it looks like to not. He listed evidence in our lives to help describe the way we *live*. I always key in on the word *live*. I want the person to be honest with who they are and how they live their lives.

I will often ask which side seems to best describe their lives. I may suggest that if they are unsure of which side of the line their life lies, people around them could help. "What do you think your spouse, friends, dating partner, parents, or coworkers would say?" This often causes some true reflection.

While Paul's list doesn't include every sin possible, it's a great place to understand what a *sinful nature* lifestyle looks like. I often focus on the phrase, "anyone *living* that sort of life will not inherit the Kingdom of God." Moving on to the fruit of the Spirit, I don't assume they have a clue who the Holy Spirit is. But I make sure they understand the idea of what Paul meant by "fruit," or what your life produces. Even the very idea of "those who belong to Christ Jesus" may be foreign to them. Again, every conversation is different, but I try to never assume the person I am talking to has ever heard these scriptures or has any understanding of what they mean.

The New Living Translation says at the beginning of that passage, "When you follow the desires of your sinful nature, the results are very clear," while other translations say the results of how we live are "obvious." This is where I want to get some certainty about where the person stands in regard to living a life for Jesus. I often ask, "Does your life look like the first list, the sins, or the second list, the fruit?" I want them to answer for themselves. Paul said it's *obvious*. Just like those TV shows I watch, we have to identify the problem ourselves before finding the solution.

Paul referred to "how we live," as in today, as in currently.

Big difference, because if he said "if you have ever done *any* of these things," then we're all doomed. But if we are "living that sort of life," then that is who we are right now. No one can tell another person which side they live on. I have no idea. I may guess given someone's initial story, but only that person and God know for sure. Again, we are not judging or acting as the judge; we are asking God to reveal to the person who they are in Him, and that begins with understanding who the person is *apart* from Him.

We can then compare the story they've shared with what the Bible says. Many, many times their life story sounds way more like the first list of sinful living than the second. For most of us, some of those sins are all too familiar at some point in our own lives. Then, we look at the other side. When explaining "fruit of the Spirit," I like to draw a tree with fruit on it. If they are going to make a decision to follow Jesus, this may be their first lesson on how to read the Bible and apply it to their life.

When Paul said, "Anyone living [a sinful] life will not inherit the Kingdom of God," this is where he drew the line. Are you *this* or are you *that*? These terms are very clear, unlike answers I often hear such as, "I'm not sure where I'm at" or "I hope I go to heaven, who knows?" Left unchanged, those lives will never be spiritually productive, and those people will never tell anyone else the Good News, because they are not sure themselves.

By this point, they're hopefully beginning to gain clarity as to which side of the line they are on. I try not to flood them with too much information or Scripture. If Paul's description of the sinful life hits a nerve, they will realize they have a problem. If they know they have a problem, I can show them answers in the Bible. And now, they are reading the Bible for themselves. I'm just the messenger, the Gospeler. Life change could be near, with a brand-new way to live.

Crossing that line goes from death to life, dark to light, lost to found. The Bible offers many words describing the before and after. But it is a line that's crossed. It's an in-or-out situation, just like the clear line between the two lives in Galatians 5. Think about asking someone if they're married. What if the person answers, "I'm not sure," or "I hope I am," or "I haven't thought about that in a long time," when the answer should be a clear yes or no? Answers like "We're separated," or "I was married, but now I'm divorced," or "We live together, so not officially" also offer their own answers. People tend to not like hard lines being drawn, because when life is looked at honestly, we often see we need to change. That can be scary. But change is exactly what makes people's lives look different.

THE WOMAN AT THE ROOM

Alyssa came back! She showed up to the church building the next Sunday. She did not come to the First Step room, but a lady who saw her there that day spoke to her. She told her how happy she was to see her again. To the woman's surprise, Alyssa had tears streaming down her face, saying, "I didn't take the medication I needed that morning and I'm so embarrassed by some of the things I said. I also didn't realize that was Willie Robertson." The lady assured her that I was only there to help anyone who came into that room and there were no wrong answers to any of her questions.

Alyssa then said, "I'm just desperately looking for a community who could love me."

And perhaps for the first time in her thirty years, she had found that.

> The Spirit of the Sovereign Lord is on me,
> because the Lord has anointed me
> to proclaim good news to the poor.
> He has sent me to bind up the brokenhearted,
> to proclaim freedom for the captives
> and release from darkness for the prisoners.
>> (Isaiah 61:1)

Five

GRACE RAPPELER

KORIE'S FAVORITE TIME OF THE ENTIRE YEAR IS OUR FAMILY'S ANNUAL ski trip. Because she's been snow skiing since she was a kid, it's always been an adventure for her as well as a pleasant reminder of her past when she first learned to glide down mountain runs, skiing with her family and warming up with hot cocoa after a long day on the slopes. It's my wife's winter wonderland heaven on earth.

When it's time for us to go skiing, I can assure you I have none of the warm and fuzzy memories Korie does. Just reminders. I am reminded that the altitude will make me sick and dizzy for the first few days. I am reminded that what begins as a runny nose will turn into a wicked sinus infection, marked by my nose blowing out a strange-looking artwork that resembles a CSI shotgun blast. I am reminded of the beautiful way my lungs scream for more oxygen, as I often have to stop after taking only five or six steps in the thin mountain air.

I am also reminded of my disdain for trying on clothes.

Our wonderful family tradition always seems to require me to try on all my equipment alongside twenty-plus people, one . . . at . . . a . . . time. Then if you get it wrong in this trying-on process, you're guaranteed to be miserable the entire time you are "enjoying" your ski vacation. Because a wrong clothing choice could result in burning up with sweat even though you're in sub-freezing temps, or freezing to death *because* of the sweat. A wrong boot choice can leave pain and bruising on shins that lasts for days. Korie's little piece of heaven on the hills is my dizzy-can't-breathe-freezing-sweating-nightmare hell on earth.

It's weird how this mountaintop experience can be viewed so differently by two people who live in agreement about most everything else in life the rest of the year! Korie sees a mountain and wonders how quickly she can get to the top to fly back down, while I am totally satisfied being at the bottom with my oxygen tank and Vaseline for my nose. She finds joy in the coming-down-really-fast part, while I just see a knee injury waiting to happen. Or a sinus infection. Or a mountain rescue team having to rappel down a cliff to come get me, with all their ropes and equipment.

While those rescue squads are pretty impressive, I hope I never have to meet them in action on a mountain. Thankfully, having Korie's level of enthusiasm for skiing isn't a requirement for getting rescued. Whether you're a veteran like my wife or a novice like me, it's comforting to know they will come if anything happens.

But the contrast of Korie and me is exactly what I have seen over and over through my years of sharing Jesus. Just like we have different attitudes toward the mountain, with different childhoods and memories, people have different reactions toward Jesus. With so many types of people, from all kinds of backgrounds and ages, you never know how they're going to react to hearing about Him. It could be because of their past faith experience, for better or worse, or their knowledge or lack of understanding of the Bible. The outcome can be all over the map in how people respond when told about Jesus.

No matter what, though, Jesus is there for them. He's the rescue squad. It doesn't matter if a person is receptive to hearing about Jesus, wants nothing to do with Him, or is anywhere in between. The truth is, for all people, He's there to save us. He comes when we call out to Him for rescue. You could call Jesus the Grace Rappeler.

God's Son came down to earth to provide grace for the human race, to offer rescue to the lost and hopeless. He became a man and lived among His creation. He was executed by the very people He created, was buried in the same way people honor their dead, but came back to life on the third day. That's the big difference between Jesus and the rest of us; without Him we can't come back to life. But He did, and He rescues us so that we can have eternal life with Him. That's the Good News of the Gospel. And it's good whether you grew up loving Jesus since you were a child or you find yourself a grown man stuck on the side of the mountain in need of rescue. He comes down and offers grace to all who call on His name.

> I lift up my eyes to the mountains—
> where does my help come from?
> My help comes from the LORD,
> the Maker of heaven and earth.
> (Psalm 121:1–2)

Jesus came straight down from heaven to save us. Like a skilled rappeler with every stake, rope, and step carefully planned out, He was very methodical and prayerful with His life and ministry, walking every step in obedience to God's plan. Each stake was put in just the right place at just the right time to reach the goal that He came to earth to accomplish. Everything was carefully aligned toward the cross and the empty tomb. In a world where we are all trying to race to the top, Jesus' mission was all about coming down from heaven to rescue and redeem.

GETTING TO THE HEART

For the message of the cross is foolishness to those who are perishing, but to us who are being saved it is the power of God. (1 Corinthians 1:18)

To be rescued by Jesus is far greater than a mountain rescue by the ski patrol. When Jesus rappels into your life, not only does your day-to-day life change but your life for eternity is set. But why do people sometimes react like it's not that big of a deal? I believe there are a few main reasons.

One of the problems with dropping the Good News of Jesus into a conversation today is that many folks feel like it's old news. They've heard it all before. Perhaps even tried it. Like when you start telling someone a story, and the person lets you know immediately, "Oh, yeah, I know this one" or "Yeah, I've heard all about that. No need to continue telling it." (Of course, that doesn't always work to stop someone. My parents often tell me stories I've heard a hundred times, and I no longer bother trying to stop them.)

The Good News is often packaged with so many rules, traditions, and rituals that for a lot of people the true meaning of the Gospel has been drowned in religion. Many have forgotten the real reason Jesus came down to earth in the first place. Some realize after a quick conversation that they don't actually know much about Him at all. As I listen to people's stories, it's important to hear how they may view God, Jesus, the church, and what they've been through. But my only goal is to share the Good News with them—the rescue. Once again, the Gospel has the power; I just need to share it with them.

> **I DON'T WANT TO JUST GIVE SOMEONE INFORMATION. I WANT THEM TO CONSIDER SURRENDERING TO JESUS.**

When trying to explain the Gospel to someone, you can't think, *Well, I'll just tell them what Jesus did and that should do the trick.* You want the person to listen, engage, and take the story to heart and enter into a relationship that's life-changing. It's not just the knowledge that saves; even Satan knows who Jesus is. James 2:19 states, "Even the demons believe this, and they tremble in terror" (NLT). The knowledge scares them! So, I don't want to just give someone information. I want them to consider surrendering to Jesus, something demons *never* want to do.

Back to the difference between Korie and me on the ski slopes. I know how to ski; I have taken the lessons. I get the mechanics of it, but I don't love it, and I'm not going to do it willingly. Korie loves it. Being a skier has become part of who she is, and you might say she has a relationship with the mountain. She is willing to do the hard work, to overcome whatever pain or inconvenience might go along with it because she loves it. There's a big difference in knowing about something or someone and loving something or someone. One changes what you know; the other changes how you live.

> And pray for me, too. Ask God to give me the right words so I can boldly explain God's mysterious plan that the Good News is for Jews and Gentiles alike. (Ephesians 6:19 NLT)

Why was Paul asking for prayers to have "the right words" to explain the Good News even clearer, when he knew the Gospel better than anyone? In every unique situation, Paul wanted God to give him specifically what that person needed for understanding. Not just to download the facts into their heads but to help them begin to see the "mysterious plan" of the Good News. The real connection. That's why we can't make any assumptions about what people may know, even if it seems like they know a lot *about* God.

For example, a whole bunch of folks know *about* me, but they really don't know *me*. They got a sense of who I am from watching *Duck Dynasty* every week, or who they think I am, but they don't *know* me. They don't live with me every day to see every side of who I am. TV Willie is one-dimensional; everyday Willie is three-dimensional. I once had a huge guy come at me like he was going to grab me in a bear hug. I put out my hand and said, "Hey, remember, I don't know you!"

Like I said, I try not to make any assumptions about whether a person actually knows Jesus. I can tell you from experience that a lot of people know *of* Him, but truly knowing Jesus is a whole other thing. When a Gospeler shares the Good News with someone, they should pray that the Spirit leads that person into a relationship with Jesus.

OF FIRST IMPORTANCE

After I have gathered a person's story and walked through Galatians 5 to talk about the two ways of living—by the acts of the sinful nature or by the Spirit—I am ready to talk about Jesus. As a reminder, I think it's important to have people read these scriptures. You want them to see the Bible as the guide, the place where they find the answers. I know we don't have the time to read all of Matthew, Mark, Luke, and John, so I want them to know what the Gospel is in its simplest, purest form. That's why that particular passage is so good in explaining the difference in just a few sentences.

Next, I head to my favorite chapter in the New Testament, which is 1 Corinthians 15 because it reminds me of a pep talk by a great football coach. Paul was writing to a group of believers, but I've found it can be great for someone who may not believe at all. Especially when I talk to folks who have a lot of religious mumbo-jumbo baggage clouding who Jesus is and what the Gospel means, I like to go to this passage of Scripture because it takes the conversation straight to what is of "first importance."

> For what I received I passed on to you as of first importance:
> that Christ died for our sins according to the Scriptures.
> (1 Corinthians 15:3)

Pretty simple, right? Yet we make it so complicated.

Korie says the main thing about skiing is to just point your skis down the mountain and enjoy the scenery. It seems a lot more complicated than that to me. I'm a golfer, so I think of it like this: Sometimes when beginning a relationship with Jesus, we're like the guy who is trying to keep everything he's been taught in mind as he learns to swing a golf club. He gets in an awkward stance and tells himself, "Okay, left arm straight, back upright, hips out of the way, don't move my head, keep the triangle, get back to the same position you start at the ball, follow through on the swing, and finish with my chest toward the target. Don't grip the club too tightly. . . . Oh, and don't forget to breathe!"

Then he draws back and whacks the dirt behind the ball, and it goes only a few feet. Perhaps he assumed he would automatically be a good golfer because his mom or dad was a great golfer. However, with all the noise in his head, he forgot the main thing—to actually hit the ball! You will never be good at golf if you can't do that, but once you can consistently connect with the ball, you have a starting point.

It's the same with the Gospel: If you don't start with Jesus, it will not work. Like the new golfer, you can't say, "Okay, go to church every Sunday, small group every Tuesday night, give money, don't mess up, always do the right thing, pray every morning, read the Bible every night, and follow all the rules. . . . Oh, and don't forget to breathe!" None of these things will be productive unless you are introduced to Jesus and understand what He did for you right from the start: He came down from heaven and died for your sins so you could be rescued and free. You have to stay focused on the main thing—Jesus.

Let's jump into more of chapter 15:

> Now, brothers and sisters, I want to remind you of the gospel I preached to you, which you received and on which you have taken your stand. By this gospel you are saved, if you hold firmly to the word I preached to you. Otherwise, you have believed in vain. For what I received I passed on to you as of first importance: that Christ died for our sins according to the Scriptures, that he was buried, that he was raised on the third day according to the Scriptures. (vv. 1–4)

In Lee Strobel's book *The Case for Christ*, he singles out this very passage as one of the oldest in the New Testament.[1] I was excited when I read his research on this scripture. Turns out it's a vital passage packed with great truths. Paul let this group know the importance of the Gospel. I love how he spelled out all the ideas around it before he even revealed exactly what it was. Years ago, I committed this passage to memory, and I have quoted it often when discussing faith with others.

This is also the Scripture passage my father and mother would read all those years ago as they contemplated where their life was headed. These verses can give the proper framework of what should be the most important thing in our lives—the Gospel, the Good News of Jesus Christ. In verse 3, Paul said, "I passed on to you as of first importance," basically meaning, "Hey! Don't miss this!"

We talk about things that are important to us, right? If it's not that important, we don't bring it up much. But if people can't seem to shut us up about something, everyone knows it's a huge deal in our lives. It's like Paul was making sure his audience did not miss the real reason why we live this way. Again, that's why when I gather someone's story, I first listen to what's important to the person, then I share this scripture that tells us what should be of first importance in all our lives.

> JESUS, THE GRACE RAPPELER, CAME DOWN AND DIED FOR OUR SINS SO WE COULD BE SAVED AND HAVE A RELATIONSHIP WITH HIM.

Jesus, the Grace Rappeler, came down and died for our sins so we could be saved and have a relationship with Him. That's the heart of it, and when we share the Gospel, that's of first importance.

In verse 1, Paul said it was "the gospel I preached to you, which you received and on which you have taken your stand." When I'm in conversations, I have no idea if the person has received the Gospel at all. Like I said, I try to not make any assumptions—that could be a big turnoff to someone and become an obstacle to their hearing it. But if I find out they have received it, everything shifts and *we* have a lot to share. If they haven't, *I* have much to share.

MAKING YOUR STAND

The original cover art for our TV show had the subtitle under *Duck Dynasty* as "Money, Family, Ducks." When I saw that, I understood the network didn't yet know us very well. Thousands of cards had been printed with that line above our picture for us to autograph at events. Of course, we didn't like money being one of our core descriptors, because it's not. So we made a stand on the Gospel.

Every single time we signed one of those cards, we drew an X across *money* and above it wrote *FAITH*. In our version, faith would always be first. This was a way of declaring the Gospel over how the network wanted us to be portrayed. Like I said—"of first importance."

Going back to the first verse of 1 Corinthians 15, think about starting a faith conversation with, "How do you make your stand on the Gospel?" Now *that* would be a target question that could get to the heart of the matter quickly! There are times throughout our lives when we need to ask that question to ourselves too. With everything that comes at us in everyday life, it can be tough to stay focused on what's "of first importance."

In the next verse, Paul talked about the reason we can make our stand. He said, "By this gospel you are saved." The line begins to form between the two lives we might live: saved or lost, alive or dead, free or captive, in light or in darkness. This is the point in the conversation that each person will draw their own conclusion about where they are standing in relationship to the Gospel.

Paul's next sentences say, "If you hold firmly to the word I preached to you. Otherwise, you have believed in vain." I find that super interesting. Paul dropped two qualifiers—*if* and *otherwise*. Why? Because he knew very well that there is a surrender that must happen when someone decides to follow Jesus. Some hear the gospel and come in hot but flame out. Oftentimes, this is why we must have these conversations. Many have heard of Jesus, but over time they don't hold firm to what they were taught.

Jesus acknowledged that problem in the parable of the

sower. In it, He told us that the seed of the Gospel is like a farmer who sows seed all over, but where it lands determines whether it takes root and grows.

> Then he told them many things in parables, saying: "A farmer went out to sow his seed. As he was scattering the seed, some fell along the path, and the birds came and ate it up. Some fell on rocky places, where it did not have much soil. It sprang up quickly, because the soil was shallow. But when the sun came up, the plants were scorched, and they withered because they had no root. Other seed fell among thorns, which grew up and choked the plants. Still other seed fell on good soil, where it produced a crop—a hundred, sixty or thirty times what was sown. Whoever has ears, let them hear." (Matthew 13:3–9)

The sower never knows when the soil is going to be just right. And sometimes you just have to keep sowing in the same spot.

RIPE FOR HARVEST

A few years back, a good friend of mine started having some health issues. On a CT scan of his brain, numerous spots showed up, so doctors scheduled surgery to see what they were up against. To me, this was really bad news, because I had tried to share Jesus with him on multiple occasions without good results. Now I felt an urgency due to his scary and uncertain diagnosis.

I sensed that my friend Bill was a guy who didn't have the Gospel as a priority in his life. As I read him Galatians 5, many of those attributes of a life without God seemed obvious. But he had a particular way of responding. Every time I brought up something spiritual, he'd quote from John 8: "Let he who hath not sinned cast the first stone." This felt less like knowledge of the Word and more like, "Get off my back. I don't want to hear what you have to say about God or my life." I never let responses like these bother me. My job is simply to share and wait for God to open the door.

Yet, even with his diagnosis, he didn't seem concerned with the reality of his own mortality. I don't know much about spots on the brain, but they usually are not good in any way. I was going to have to get creative if my friend was going to hear the Good News of Jesus from me. I was not going to let this be the end of it. I had to keep trying, sowing, for Bill's sake.

He was a very successful businessman, so financial discussions would come up from time to time. He knew I didn't want his money, which always helps when sharing the Gospel with a wealthy person. People of means can tend to be very distrustful, especially when someone is toting a Bible. Sad, but true. For years we had many conversations, but he would always steer away from anything deep. I got the sense he needed Jesus more than ever, but I couldn't break through his tough shell to get to the heart of the matter. I needed the Spirit to do the hard work of creating that opening—of preparing the soil.

We were in New York together for business in the back of a Suburban being driven into Midtown from a meeting we had just finished outside the city. He was rattling off numbers and going over the deal when I decided it was time for me to not just *look* for an opportunity but *make* an opportunity to get the Gospel to him.

At the time, Bill not only had been diagnosed with tumors

on his brain, but he also smoked like a freight train, which I knew had to be affecting his health. Looking straight at him, I asked one simple question: "How old are you?"

"Fifty-seven," he popped back, looking sort of curious.

I thought for a second and then stated, "I think you'll be dead in fourteen years. Have you ever thought about what you're investing in *this* life to prepare for life *after* this?"

> IT WAS TIME FOR ME TO NOT JUST *LOOK* FOR AN OPPORTUNITY BUT *MAKE* AN OPPORTUNITY TO GET THE GOSPEL TO HIM.

Honestly, I had no idea where this line of questions came from outside of the Holy Spirit handing it to me. I certainly hadn't planned it. I just knew all the methods I had used in the past always led him to quote, "He who hath not sinned . . ." So I went with death and investments. I could see right away I hit a nerve. He looked at me with eyes wide open. Guess what he didn't say this time?

"I've never thought about that," he answered. His whole countenance changed. He seemed nervous, then asked, "Do you really think that's all the time I have left?"

I told him I wasn't sure but that his time was definitely coming. By that point, we had pulled up to the hotel. He asked if I could come to his room to continue talking. I went to my room, grabbed my Bible, and joined him. When I walked in, his wife was there in the suite with him. She was in the bedroom, and we sat down on the couch in the living area.

Just as I do every time, the first thing I did was listen to his story. Finally, he was ready to talk about it. He told me he had come to faith in college. But over the years of building businesses and life moving fast, he had not "held firmly to the Gospel." His life didn't look like the one where the fruit of the Spirit pours out; it was more like the other side. As I was showing him responses to the Gospel in the New Testament, his moment happened. Grace rappelled down into that hotel room! For the first time in his life, Bill fully surrendered his life to Jesus. He stood to his feet and yelled to his wife in the other room, "I'm getting baptized!" She shouted back, "That's great!"

Then he said, "You need to as well!"

I looked at him and said, "Well, Bill, it's around midnight in New York City. I can go see if I can find some water."

To which he replied, "No, not tonight. I have to tell everyone I know. I want them all to be there to witness it."

I encouraged him to keep in touch, and the next day, I left to go back home.

It's always good when people have to keep searching. The Gospel will do that. It hits people in different ways. My father took months to finally let go and start his journey with Jesus at the helm. For Bill, I had been throwing seeds in this same spot for years, and finally I was able to see a leaf spring up.

Later, I traveled to California with Bill and his wife on a plane and shared with them for hours about the Good News of Jesus Christ. A month or so after that, Bill called me with a date and location for his baptism. He wanted to be baptized in a lake on his property in Louisiana. His wife had decided she wanted to be baptized too, but she preferred a blow-up pool rather than getting in the lake on that cold November day.

Bill had everything set up. When I got there, I was immediately struck by the number of vehicles. He had done exactly what he said he would do, telling everyone about this special occasion. There were people there from LA to New York—lawyers, restaurant and bar owners, businesspeople, family, and friends from all over.

But little did I know he had more in mind for his audience. Bill was making his stand.

He gathered everyone up in the backyard and announced, "Willie, tell them what you told me in that hotel room in New York City!"

I started with 1 Corinthians 15 and told them the story of Jesus. I talked about how Bill and his wife wanted to change their lives by living for Jesus, how Bill didn't want his belief to be "in vain." When I was done, we started in the kiddie pool with his wife, Beth. After she was baptized, everyone cheered. After Beth, their daughter and a friend who was pregnant went next.

Then the whole group followed Bill and me down the hill to the lake. When he came up out of the water, he raised his hands in a true victory formation and squeezed me in a giant hug. Then Bill looked at the group standing on the bank and shouted, "Whoever is next, come on in!"

Then the miraculous happened. The remarkable took place. Something I did not see coming. People started streaming into that lake. They waded into the water in their dress shirts and jeans, fully clothed, one after another. They just kept coming. By the time we were done, twenty-four people had responded to the Gospel by committing their lives to Jesus and getting baptized. *Amazing. Only God.*

I had brought a friend with me to record this special time. I hired Jordan right out of college to be the cameraman for my hunting shows. He shared with me how much he was impacted by what he had seen. Turns out he had doubts about his own faith. He realized he had never made Jesus his Lord. After many tears and a prayer, one more was baptized in the middle of the night in a swimming pool. Number twenty-five.

Think about this for a moment. Had I given up on Bill after the first time I shared with him because of his constant "He who hath not sinned" quotes, at least on that day, those folks would not have had the opportunity to make their decisions and turn their life to Christ. I had no idea that my many tries and the "risk" I took of telling him he had fourteen years left would lead to so many people responding to the Gospel. It's just more evidence that we have to be faithful to share, to not give up, and to trust that God will provide the power. That's what I want you to see about this story—it's not about what I did with my friend but about what God did in the lives of twenty-five people in just a few hours!

You can see why it's so important for people to have a reminder of what the Gospel is all about. Paul told us that our sin was paid in full by the death of Jesus on a cross. Then He was buried. But the best part of the Good News is the last part. He came back from the dead. Without that, we would have no hope of living again. He showed us His power while humbly displaying His servanthood at the same time. The resurrection is the big news that makes this the Good News! The resurrection is the game changer! Remember that Jesus Himself had confronted Paul on the road to Damascus, so Paul was speaking from personal experience. In fact, he was temporarily blinded by the sight of the *risen* Jesus.

The very fact that Paul was reminding the Corinthians of the Gospel lets me know how important it is to always keep telling others about Jesus. My entire family was changed because of the story of what He did. Bill and his family all chose to follow Jesus, so a new Gospel genealogy was created in their family too. Since that day, not a week has gone by that I don't get a question about a scripture from someone in their family.

In Matthew 28, Jesus' final commission to His disciples was plain and simple:

> Then Jesus came to them and said, "All authority in heaven and on earth has been given to me. Therefore go and make disciples of all nations, baptizing them in the name of the Father and of the Son and of the Holy Spirit, and teaching them to obey everything I have commanded you. And surely I am with you always, to the very end of the age." (vv. 18–20)

- Go to all nations.
- Make disciples.
- Baptize them in My name.
- Teach them to obey everything I taught you.

He started with the authority that had been given to Him to make this commission and ended with a reminder that He would always be present with them through the Holy Spirit. So there is nothing special about us; it's all about Him. We don't have to add a bunch of other information, incentives, or requirements to the Gospel for it to be compelling to people. We also shouldn't take anything away from it. But we can get as creative as we want to get folks to stop and think about what the Gospel is and how it can change their lives. Paul even said that he became "all things to all people so that by all possible means [he] might save some" (1 Corinthians 9:22).

Many times, just our own personal testimonies of what Jesus has done can be powerful for others. Hearing about other people's problems and struggles can be comforting when you realize you are not alone in your struggles. We may have faced the same types of issues, but we have found a real Answer.

When a rescue team is doing their job, they are trying to save someone in danger and bring them to safety and security, and then they tend to their injuries. That's exactly what Jesus did as the Rescuer, bringing God's grace to us. He descended to save us. Jesus—the Grace Rappeler—invites each of us to join Him now, today and for eternity. It's His great love that heals our wounds.

"For the Son of Man came to seek and to save the lost."
(Luke 19:10)

Six

BIBLE DETAILER

IN 2020, KORIE AND I SIGNED UP TO DO A SHOW WITH FACEBOOK (PRE-
Meta). With everything going on with the COVID pandemic and
all the division in our country, we wanted to try to deal with
some tough issues in a talk show format. Our goal was to demonstrate that people can have differences but still be friends, or
at least be friendly and kind toward one another in a respect-
ful discussion. None of the yelling and screaming that seems
to really sell these days. We wanted to have people in our home
who may disagree on a topic try to find common ground, and
thought that tackling such a big task on a huge platform was
certainly worth a try.

We felt great about the show and all the people we met. We
had meaningful and positive conversations, covering issues
like racism, gun control, kneeling during the national anthem,
COVID vaccinations, and even vegan versus meat diets. With
some guests, we ended up agreeing, and with others, we just
agreed to disagree. Regardless of the guest and the topic, we listened and we learned.

One of the hardest parts of having these kinds of conversations in our country is that there is no longer a clear standard of truth. "Truth" today is most often based on people's personal assumptions, opinions, current feelings, or their own understanding or misunderstanding of an issue. That's why the buzz phrase has become "my truth," meaning a person has chosen a position and no one can disagree with or challenge it. It's not *the* truth or even *a* truth, but *my* truth. Then the extreme reaction comes when *any* pushback at all is considered to be hatred. An all-or-none mentality.

Today, some folks think America is inherently bad, while others think it's the greatest nation on earth. Still others feel that it's a bit of both. Oftentimes, this mindset is being driven by issues like passion, pain, abuse, or injustice. Ironically, while we all seem to feel like change is needed, it's a rarity these days to agree on what that change actually looks like.

That's why it has become so easy to camp out with like-minded folks and tune out the rest of the world. Circle the wagons and shoot on sight. Honestly, that's what we see more and more people doing. They don't really talk *to* each other. They talk *at* each other. They talk *about* each other. Some have no idea how or where they formed their beliefs in the first place, because they just went with the crowd.

Even science isn't always to be trusted today. For so long, many people felt like that was the gold standard, as in "That's not *my* opinion, that's science!" As a fan of the TV show *Dateline*, I love when they bring in the scientist to testify on a case to give an expert opinion. I hear the testimony and think, *Checkmate!* Then the other side brings in their scientist and totally refutes the first scientist! That's when I'm confused and think, *They both seem convincing, so where's the truth?*

All these reasons are why I use the Bible as my guide and standard. I find comfort in knowing there is one place where I can find truth. When I talk to people about their lives, that's always where I'm going to end up looking for answers. Not my truth or the person's truth, but God's truth. Because I believe Him and His Word. I believe Jesus is God and came to earth to pay for our sins. I believe the Spirit of God is alive and living in those who choose God through Jesus. And I will tell others what I believe until the day I die and move on from this earth. It's what I believe. I *can't* change that. I *won't* change that. That's also the very reason I have learned to pay attention to the details in the Bible—all the specifics and fine points that we find in every story and conversation in Scripture.

For example, in over thirty years of communication, some of the biggest arguments Korie and I have had have been over details that were missed, overlooked, forgotten, or we spent way too much time on. I believe that's why many marriages end—because spouses start to ignore or forget all those details they once agreed were important.

Because details are so important to someone's faith decision, I never get too far away from the Bible when I'm talking to people. In fact, we have to be careful to not let a religious mindset or personal agenda start to override details from the Bible and begin to create a whole new batch of information that doesn't matter; the kind of details that come from men tend to become methods. And before you know it, we spend more time on the *methods* and completely miss the *message*. That's exactly what Jesus was up against with the Pharisees and Sadducees. That's why, no matter how old-fashioned or outdated the Bible may sound to people in our modern world, it remains my only source of truth. The method *and* message in one place.

STABLE STANDARD

One summer night I was sitting around a campfire and wanted to have a conversation with a young man there who considered himself an atheist. I was told he had no belief in God, so I was praying and devising a plan to share the Good News with him. The other guys were just chitchatting, so I positioned my chair by his and started asking questions. He let me know quickly that he did not believe in God or the Bible. Ready for that response, I continued.

As I was trying to get his story, right at the worst moment, a guy sitting on the other side of the fire blurted out, "You need to believe in God 'cuz it's in the Bible!" I knew this aggressive tone was not the way to open this young man's mind and heart. So I ignored the comment, switched gears, and asked about his family. About that time, the guy tried again: "Jesus is in the Bible! You gotta believe in Jesus if you wanna go to heaven!" After that, I knew I was going to have to stop the heckling from the peanut gallery. This was exactly the type of stuff this young man had rejected his whole life.

I pointedly told our friend, "He doesn't *believe* in the Bible, so you can stop saying it's *in* the Bible!" The guy finally got the message and didn't chime in again.

I knew the young man was married, so I said, "Tell me about your wife."

HIM: We just got married a year ago.

ME: That's awesome, congrats. So, what's your hesitation about believing in God?

HIM: I only have faith in what I can see . . . I don't know who wrote the Bible. I wasn't there and neither were you. That's why I don't believe in God or the Bible.

He stated this strongly as if there was no other possible answer, so I decided to go back to his marriage.

ME: Is it possible that your wife is with another man right now? Is it possible that while you're with all us guys, she's with a guy in your absence?

HIM: No!

He answered sharply, obviously annoyed, not just by the question but by the very thought.

ME: Why not?

HIM: Because I trust her! That's why!

ME: Well, then you *do* have faith in something you can't see with your very own eyes!

Thinking for a moment, he sheepishly responded,

HIM: Okay, I guess I *do* have faith.

I decided to stop there. Enough for one night. One little victory for breaking down an idea he had built his entire life on. Now there was a crack in his disbelief, one that could allow the Gospel to flow into his life. He may not have declared the Bible as a standard that night, but if he could trust in his wife, could he trust in something even greater? He may go on to have children someday, and maybe that will open another door to a spiritual journey. I bring up marriage and family quite a bit because the Bible uses both to help us understand our relationship with God.

I'm sharing this story for two reasons: First, the details of his life were important to how I tried to engage with him, and second, in every unique circumstance we have to discern when we are seed sowers and when we are harvesters. This was clearly a sowing situation. I knew I had to create a new question in his mind about God before he would ever be open to any answer. The standard or foundation we come from is crucial to what we believe or don't believe. Korie told me one time, "Your father didn't put rules on you and your brothers like most parents do. They just hotwired you to God." She had a great point. Phil would tell us, "Do what the Bible says and we won't have any problems." He would rarely tell us to do something just because *he* said, and he would always reference a scripture.

> IN EVERY UNIQUE CIRCUMSTANCE WE HAVE TO DISCERN WHEN WE ARE SEED SOWERS AND WHEN WE ARE HARVESTERS.

With that being my parents' standard, so much of my life has been guided by the Bible. When I would hear an idea or thought, I would go see what the Word had to say about it. We have to take people from where they are. If a person doesn't believe the Bible is the Word of God, how else can we reach them? Jesus used parables to help us understand big truths. Everything in creation points to Him.

Of course, when reading the Bible, we have to account for the culture in the days it was written. We also have to pay attention to what was written in the Old Testament, then the Gospels, then Acts, all the letters to the early churches, and the Revelation from John. The details of Scripture are very helpful to know. Finding out more about who was writing and to whom it was written can help our understanding.

There have been many great books written on the validity of the Bible, with tons of historical information and evidence. There are deep intellectual minds who need those studies to crack them open to faith. I know because I have run into quite a few of those folks over the years. But I work to keep my conversations inside the lane of my own experience and knowledge. There's nothing worse than someone who has no idea what they're talking about trying to explain something to someone else. That's exactly why the guy sitting across the fire was only making matters worse and wouldn't get anywhere with the young man who proclaimed to have no faith. With talking about the things of God, there is no "fake it 'til you make it." That's why my focus in this book is what I know best—the Gospel of Jesus.

As I told you in the first chapter, I have always had a heart to teach others about Jesus. My grades were always average, but I'm way more street smart than book smart. Like most people, with the things I am passionate about, I tend to want to learn more. When I read in the Great Commission where Jesus said to go, make disciples, and baptize (Matthew 28:16–20), I knew I could tell others what Jesus did for me, but when He then said, "teaching them to obey everything I have commanded you" (v. 20), I knew I was going to have to learn the Bible. I needed to know what it says and how to apply it. I had to study as well as read, and that's something I continue to do every day.

I'm grateful that the New Testament is clear about how God used ordinary men like me to accomplish extraordinary things through the Spirit.

> When they saw the courage of Peter and John and realized that they were unschooled, ordinary men, they were astonished and they took note that these men had been with Jesus.
> (Acts 4:13)

If He can use regular people like Peter and John and me, He can certainly use you. Peter and John got to literally be with Jesus, and we get to do that through His Word and through His Spirit. Knowing the details of the Bible is key to knowing Jesus and telling His story.

WHATEVER IT TAKES

One time I was staying at the home of a pro athlete, and we were visiting together. I soon got the feeling he needed the Gospel in his life. I was struggling to find the right words to say when I got a nudge to do something I had never done before. As I was getting ready to leave, I knew I needed to give him my Bible. This was no ordinary copy, but *my* Bible. My personal Bible. The one I had carried since I was a small child. The one I had taken to school, marked up, highlighted, and used to share with countless people throughout my life. The thought of parting with something so special made me a little sad, but I had to trust God that the gift would be worth the sacrifice.

I left a note with my Bible, telling him, "This book has all the answers to your problems." Of course, I had no idea whether he would read it. I really didn't know what was going to happen, because I hadn't tried *this* before. A while after I got home, he and his wife called. They were very emotional. They could not believe the gesture. He said over and over, "Willie, I can't keep this incredible gift." But I insisted. He then asked, "So, when can you come back? I have no idea where to start in this book." So I booked another flight in hopes that the Gospel could do what only it can do—change his and his wife's hearts and the trajectory of their family for eternity.

When I returned, the conversation was now set up perfectly. He had a Bible, and he was eager to understand how its words could help him live a better life. I started, just like I always do, by getting some backstory on him. As we talked about his faith journey, I realized there was none. I mean zero. Never been to church. Never had a spiritual experience. After I read the Galatians 5 passage and the list of sins, I asked him, "Would any of those describe your life?" His eyes got big as he answered, "Yeah, Willie, all of them!"

So I figured when he heard the Good News of Jesus, it would certainly be welcome. His career had brought him fame and fortune, but it couldn't get him out of the mess those things had made of his life. Next, we read 1 Corinthians 15, a chapter about the resurrection, which showed him how Jesus was his way out of this hopeless, empty life he had been living, how Jesus had paid the price for all the disobedience he had just confessed, how Jesus came back from the dead to show guys like him and me that we, too, could live again. My friend was soaking it all up like a sponge. For the first time, he was receptive to what the Bible says and was seeing how it could apply to *his* life.

Because he had never even opened a Bible, he had no context of what to do. He didn't know how it started or ended. So to help him get a perspective, I took the Bible and separated it at the Old Testament and New Testament. I wasn't going to walk through Adam and Eve, Jewish history, all the prophets, and everything else that led up to Jesus. I had a man with problems who needed to simply hear that Jesus is the answer. As quickly as possible, we needed to get to verses like John 14:6: "Jesus answered, 'I am the way and the truth and the life. No one comes to the Father except through me.'"

I gave him a quick tutorial of the first four books of the New Testament—the Gospels—Jesus' life from birth to death, then His resurrection. From Christmas to Easter, which he understood. Soon, my friend was caught up on the life of Jesus and was also very aware of what his own life looked like without Jesus.

Then we came to Acts, which talks about what happened after Jesus left the earth in physical form. That book has always piqued my interest because it's the same place we are in today. Like the people in the book of Acts, we are living after the resurrection. In Acts 1, Jesus left and said to wait for the Spirit to show up to help. There would no mistaking when He came. In Acts 2 the Holy Spirit roared in, and the world has never been the same. Peter got up and addressed the crowd. The same guy who denied even knowing Jesus just a short time before. The guy Jesus sat with after He came back from the dead to make sure he knew he was needed in the kingdom of God. Jesus had told Peter his job was to feed His sheep, and now, here he was, feeding. Much like I was feeding my friend the Good News of Jesus.

Here's Peter's first public shot at being a Gospeler:

Fellow Israelites, listen to this: Jesus of Nazareth was a man accredited by God to you by miracles, wonders and signs, which God did among you through him, as you yourselves know. This man was handed over to you by God's deliberate plan and fore-knowledge; and you, with the help of wicked men, put him to death by nailing him to the cross. But God raised him from the dead, freeing him from the agony of death, because it was impossible for death to keep its hold on him. (Acts 2:22–24)

I pointed out to my friend that Peter anchored his speech with the same Gospel that Paul said is most important (1 Corinthians 15:3). I wanted him to know what it's all about, to connect the dots. If someone knows nothing about the Bible, then we need to focus on what the whole Bible is all about—the Gospel. The Old Testament is pointing to Jesus' coming, and everything after-ward points back to Him and what He came to do.

I then finished off Peter's sermon with Acts 2:37: "When the people heard this, they were cut to the heart and said to Peter and the other apostles, 'Brothers, what shall we do?'" The "this" they heard refers to the Gospel. While Peter was talking to a crowd of people, I was talking to one person in his living room. I was wanting to know if my friend was also "cut to the heart." If he understood what Jesus did for him, hopefully it would cause the same response: "Willie, what do I need to do?"

Peter answered the crowd with, "Repent and be baptized, every one of you, in the name of Jesus Christ for the forgiveness of your sins. And you will receive the gift of the Holy Spirit" (v. 38).

My buddy had no idea what those words even meant, so I knew we had to talk about the meaning of repenting. The word *repent* means "to turn from sin," "to feel regret," "to change one's mind."[1] Repentance can be a big challenge when our lives are characterized by sinful living, especially if we are known by most everyone around us by these actions.

In my father's story, it was pretty obvious that he would have to change the way he was living. I think most people know that when you enter into new things, changes have to be made. It's not a foreign concept. I'll use marriage again as an analogy. When two people get married, they can't continue living like they did when they were single. A change must be made. The real change comes when we no longer act like we once did. A married person should no longer act like a single person. Repentance can be stated with our mouths, but it is truly known only by actual change in our lives (Matthew 3:8; Acts 26:20).

We can't keep doing the same old things and expect new, different results. I wanted my friend to know that following Jesus and the Bible is not some enchanted way of life. Jesus expects no less than our spouses want in our relationship—total commitment. For this to happen, changes *must* be made.

"In the same way, those of you who do not give up everything you have cannot be my disciples." (Luke 14:33)

ON MISSION, ON MESSAGE

Before Jesus even started His mission on earth, John the Baptist cranked up his. Now, from the Bible's description of "John the baptizer," he could have been a character that fit right in on *Duck Dynasty*. Matthew 3:4 states, "John's clothes were made of camel's hair, and he had a leather belt around his waist. His food was locusts and wild honey." He came out of the wilderness with a message. He seemingly had one mission—pointing people to Jesus, the Son of God. This is the same mission we have today.

I've often joked that when *Duck Dynasty* first aired on TV, just like John the Baptist, there were these guys who came out of the woods, didn't cut their hair, wore camo, and ate weird stuff, all while pointing people to Jesus and baptizing them in the river. God has always used all sorts of people to complete His mission. Then and now, the main message is to repent and get ready for a whole new way of life. The Savior of the world is here! Just like John preached:

> "I baptize you with water for repentance. But after me comes one who is more powerful than I, whose sandals I am not worthy to carry. He will baptize you with the Holy Spirit and fire." (Matthew 3:11)

Can you imagine how hard it was for John to tell people about someone who was yet to come, with a plan for mankind that had not happened yet? That was a difficult task. There wasn't a church as we know it today, only Jewish synagogues. There were no "brothers and sisters," only Jews and Gentiles. He was a lone voice talking about God's plan for One to come who would create a new kingdom. There had been prophets before, of course, telling of a coming Messiah, but John was different: this was all happening right then and there.

> In those days John the Baptist came, preaching in the wilderness of Judea and saying, "Repent, for the kingdom of heaven has come near." (Matthew 3:1–2)

We could learn a great deal from folks like John, whose mission drives their entire life. Living with a God-given and God-driven purpose every day, he knew he had to get the message of Jesus out, no matter the cost. He would eventually be put in prison and beheaded, all *because* of the message. His short life played an important role in preparing the way for Jesus. The people who responded to John's message were not yet acting on the Gospel but were getting their lives in line with God's holiness. We're not much different today. People always have to deal with who they have been in the past before they can ever try to become something different.

> LIVING WITH A GOD-GIVEN AND GOD-DRIVEN PURPOSE EVERY DAY, HE KNEW HE HAD TO GET THE MESSAGE OF JESUS OUT, NO MATTER THE COST.

Now, back to my pro athlete friend . . .

Literally up to this moment, he had lived the life *he* wanted to live. He had done most everything he wanted to do—by any measure, a sinful life with few concessions. So why change now? Why was he looking for something different? After living just as he wanted all those years, why did he feel like something was missing? Because nothing had filled the emptiness he had, he felt a call to change from the way he had always lived.

After working through those verses with me, my friend

professed he wanted to walk with Jesus. He had seen the Word of God for himself, applied the words to his life, and decided to start a new journey. Ironically, he had just built a hot tub. So, the first time he got in it was to be baptized. From this point, I knew the road ahead would not be easy for my friend. When we have lived our lives one way for so long, it's difficult to change everything and live differently. But that was *his* new mission. *Mine* was to pass the message along to him.

In my experience, most people today have heard things about Jesus. They know He's in the Bible. They see the good in some of the people who claim to follow Him, but unfortunately, most commonly, the bad that folks do in His name is the focus. They see and hear those Christians who claim to somehow know something the rest of us don't. The ones who look at anyone who is not a believer with an angry, judgmental disposition. They see all these types of "Christians" under the same banner of faith. That was my friend's roadblock. He had always seen Christians in a bad light and was turned off by how some had treated him. But he had never read the Bible for himself. Now everything had changed. He had come into his own relationship with Jesus. The seed of the Gospel had been firmly planted in his life.

IT'S WHO YOU KNOW

Our witness to others is most often the gateway to how they find faith. The woman at the well went and told her whole town. People who believed John the Baptist when he told them a Messiah was coming got baptized in the river where he preached. This is nothing new. In business, we call that "word of mouth." But it's not just about hearing something; it's also about taking action. The "What must I do?" moment of truth when people are ready to surrender their lives to the King of kings.

Zacchaeus was a small man with a big bank account from working as a dishonest tax collector. He had heard about Jesus, and when he found out this man was coming to his town, he was curious. As Jesus came through Jericho, Zacchaeus climbed up into a tree just to get a glimpse. When Jesus looked up at him, a remarkable thing happened that Zacchaeus didn't expect. Jesus spoke directly to him. In that moment, Zacchaeus must have felt like a really big deal. The One everyone was talking about had singled him out in the crowd.

> Jesus entered Jericho and was passing through. A man was there by the name of Zacchaeus; he was a chief tax collector and was wealthy. He wanted to see who Jesus was, but because he was short he could not see over the crowd. So he ran ahead and climbed a sycamore-fig tree to see him, since Jesus was coming that way. When Jesus reached the spot, he looked up and said to him, "Zacchaeus, come down immediately. I must stay at your house today." So he came down at once and welcomed him gladly. (Luke 19:1–6)

That story reminds me of a time I will never forget—being at the State of the Union address in 2014. Korie and I were invited by a congressman and sat in the upper balcony. President Obama had given his speech and left the room. All of Congress, the Senate, and other dignitaries followed and left the floor while everyone in the balcony was told to wait. Someone was sent to find us and ask if we wanted to walk down on the floor. You mean the very floor where everything I had just witnessed had taken place? "Heck yeah!" I exclaimed.

Everyone around me was still seated as we went down and strolled the aisles on the floor. I'm sure all those people in the balcony were wondering who the homeless-looking guy was standing behind the podium where the president had just addressed the country on national TV. I have to be honest, I really thought I was something special. After we were finished looking around, we walked into a hallway. Just as I attempted to push the elevator button, a female police officer yelled at me, "Hey! You can't leave the building! The president has not left yet!"

Completely unaware of the formalities or the security measures, I apologized to her. As we stood there waiting, I looked down the hall, and there came the president and first lady, walking right toward us. They were surrounded by Secret Service and the whole entourage. I had met President Obama once before at the White House Correspondents' Dinner. Just as I was thinking to myself, *I wonder if he'll remember me*, I heard "Willie!" I looked up and realized the president himself had called out my name. He not only remembered me but walked out of the Secret Service circle, came over, and gave me a big hug!

Immediately, I was concerned that the men in black were going to ruin my big moment and take me out because I'm sure to them I looked really suspicious. With no idea if they had seen our TV show or not, I could see them scanning me up and down, like they were a heartbeat away from tackling me. After Michelle hugged Korie and the president hugged me, he smiled and graciously said, "Great to see you again."

My friends were now looking at me in a whole new way. Just

like all the townspeople of Jericho were looking up at Zacchaeus in the tree and then back at Jesus in disbelief, my friends were astonished that the president of the United States had not only recognized me but acted like we were old buddies. (Truth be told, so was I.)

As the president's entourage was walking away, I turned to the police officer who had called me out earlier and asked, "Is it okay if I leave now?" She smiled and answered, "Honey, you can do whatever you want to do!"

Now back to Jesus' new friend who was still up in a tree:

> When Jesus reached the spot, he looked up and said to him, "Zacchaeus, come down immediately. I must stay at your house today." So he came down at once and welcomed him gladly. (Luke 19:5–6)

In a moment, Zacchaeus became the biggest deal in his town. But when Jesus got to his house, I'm sure at some point it went from cool to real for the tax collector. Now he had to actually interact with this famous man everyone had been talking about. But Zacchaeus did something that I'm sure surprised everyone who knew him. Without Jesus saying a word, Zacchaeus was so overwhelmed by His acceptance and grace that, right on the spot, he vowed to change. He said to everyone that he was going to live a different life after his encounter with Jesus.

> Zacchaeus stood up and said to the Lord, "Look, Lord! Here and now I give half of my possessions to the poor, and if I have cheated anybody out of anything, I will pay back four times the amount." (Luke 19:8)

Throughout the New Testament, we see this response to Jesus over and over again: repentance—real life change. In Acts 2:40, Peter warned and pleaded with all who would listen to repent and turn from their wickedness as he cried out, "Save yourselves from this corrupt generation." John cried out, "Repent, for the kingdom of heaven has come near" (Matthew 3:2). Zacchaeus, just by being in the presence of Jesus, decided to change. He gave up his lifestyle of greed and wealth and was ready to make right the sins of his past. Just like I had to emphasize with my athlete friend, this is such an important part of the message we must tell people. Change *has* to occur. I think in our quest to get as many as possible into the kingdom, we fail them when this truth is left out.

In Luke 14:25–35, Jesus laid out the cost of becoming His disciple. In verse 31, using the analogy of a king at battle, He challenged his would-be followers to "first sit down and consider whether he is able," to make sure they fully understood the commitment a life of discipleship requires. This is not a flippant "heads bowed, eyes closed, hand in the air" gesture at the end of a religious gathering. This is not taking an "Oh, why not?" mentality about following Jesus. In fact, the question of "What have I got to lose?" is answered in verse 33: "Those of you who do not give up everything you have cannot be my disciples."

The commitment to becoming a Bible Detailer is about full surrender, commitment to change, and obedience to be more like Jesus, with His truth as your only standard. I believe we have to get back to making sure we communicate this crucial reality to anyone who hears the Gospel.

So how can the same spiritual transformation that my pro athlete friend and Zacchaeus experienced go on to create lasting change? Once again, we find the answer in the details of Jesus' words:

> "The Advocate, the Holy Spirit, whom the Father will send in my name, will teach you all things and will remind you of everything I have said to you." (John 14:26)

Part 3

RESPONSE TO THE
GOSPEL STORY

Seven

SIN CELLAR

I WAS ON A DEER HUNTING TRIP AT MY FRIEND ADAM'S PLACE IN THE Midwest. During my stay, he invited me to sit in on a weekly men's Bible study he leads at his home. There were about fifteen guys. Very casual. Someone read a passage, and then they all started to throw out comments. Since I was visiting, I didn't say much; I just listened. But I could tell this was no typical pancakes and prayer meeting.

After a while, I noticed a guy named Jake. He talked about how glad he was that he came to the group. He then shared that his original plan for the evening was to head to a local bar to "try and score a lady," but he remembered it was Bible study night, so he came to the men's meeting instead. When he finished talking, Jake got a couple of "good job" encouragements from the group.

Later, I couldn't help but ask my buddy about Jake. I wanted to know more of his story. If he was sort of flipping a coin on whether to go to the bar or the Bible study that night, I wondered if he had a real relationship with the Lord. I could be wrong, but you never know 'til you ask, right? A conversation with him could open up something. If nothing else, he would know I cared about him. So my friend agreed to ask Jake when we could talk.

We set up a hunt at Jake's place about twenty minutes away. The plan was for him to stop by and pick me up. I knew I had this one chance to bring the Good News to him, so I was not wasting any time. As I started to ask some questions to get to know him, we talked about the comments he made at the men's Bible study. Next, I asked about his spiritual life, and from Jake's answers, I could tell there was not much there. He talked about the death of a sibling, his parents' troubled marriage, and how he was baptized as a newborn. He did have some moments of spirituality in his life, but it never seemed to stick. He was hoping the men's Bible study would give him some answers in his life.

As we talked about his baptism as a baby, Jake asked me to explain more about what it meant. He wanted to know exactly what baptism is and what the Bible has to say about it. I told him about Peter telling people to repent and be baptized in Acts chapter 2. To connect the dots, I added that repentance for him might mean to stop things like going to bars to pick up women. I also talked about Paul's explanation of baptism from Romans 6:1–4. We were in his truck and I hadn't brought my Bible, so this was all very casual conversation.

After talking about a few more scriptures and hearing more of his story, we pulled up to the spot where I was going to hunt. But I could tell Jake was thinking. He sat there for a second and then declared he needed to get baptized. He said he knew his life did not look like that of a man who was following Jesus and had died to sin.

I said, "Great, go find a pool or a tub."

That's when he pointed to a cow pond out in the pasture. "We can go right there!" he said.

Now, let me give you a few important details.

This was deer season in early December in the Midwest. The temperature was right around twenty degrees *without* the windchill factor. I wasn't sure if he didn't really understand how baptism worked or whether he was just way tougher than me because he lived in this miserable cold all the time. However, if you've picked up on anything about me at all, you know I'm always up for a challenge. So I agreed we would go into the cow pond. We decided I would stay and hunt awhile first, and he would come back later to be baptized.

In a few hours, Jake showed up. He brought me a set of waders, so I knew right then he understood how this worked. I was very appreciative of his thoughtfulness, at least for my legs! After I explained what we would do once we went into the water, Jake stripped down to just some running shorts. Like a prizefighter heading into the ring, he mustered up his strength and waded in. Right there in that cow pond, in a pasture, in the middle of nowhere, in freezing cold temps, Jake declared that Jesus Christ would be the Lord of his life.

I'm not sure how much you know about cow ponds (or stock tanks as they're called in Texas and Oklahoma), but they are shallow bodies of water that cows drink from. And also stand in. And do everything else in, if you know what I mean. The one Jake and I were in was particularly shallow and, based on the smell, was a mixture of mud and manure with strong notes of urine. Trying to walk into the pond was a thigh-burning exercise as I tried to find the deepest part.

We decided quickly on the best spot, because Jake was turning a bright cherry red all over his body. He chattered out a confession to live for Jesus, and I lowered him down. As I did, I realized there was not nearly enough water where we were standing, but it was now or never. So, down he went, his face straight into the mud and manure, along with what little water was actually there. When he came up, his face literally looked like he'd seen Jesus Himself, although I believe it was mostly from the cold. There were no hugs or high-fives like usual. Jake seemed to run on water as he got out of there as quickly as possible to grab his clothes and get back to the truck.

I was tickled as I tried to break the suction of the waders so I could actually take a step. By that point, I couldn't feel my hands, so I really felt for Jake. I knew, though, that this was no casual, flippant commitment; it was a moment that would be burned into his memory forever.

Years later, as we were remembering that day, Jake shared that I was already talking about Scripture before he even turned out of the driveway. He also said it meant a lot to him that I took the time to have a conversation. Once again, I had gotten to witness the Gospel do its work in someone's life. The old Jake was put to death out in that smelly ol' sin cellar. For a lot of us, a low place full of mud and manure is actually a good metaphor for the past we are so ready to leave behind.

CONNECTING THE DOTS

Peter replied, "Repent and be baptized, every one of you, in the name of Jesus Christ for the forgiveness of your

sins. And you will receive the gift of the Holy Spirit."
(Acts 2:38)

Baptized in this verse literally means to "dip or plunge in
water."[1] Peter didn't give any explanation for this other than
naming the results of sins forgiven and the Holy Spirit received.
We know from the Gospels that John had been telling folks to get
baptized for repentance before Jesus ever arrived on the scene.
We also know Jesus was baptized by John, but now Peter was
telling people to repent and be baptized *after* Jesus had died
and come back from the dead. So baptism seems to be just as
important, if not more, to the disciples post-resurrection as it
was during Christ's earthly ministry. There are references to
baptism throughout the New Testament, but there are a lot in
the book of Acts because the early church was being established.

As I've talked to so many people just like Jake, I have noticed
that there are all sorts of ideas about what exactly baptism is or
what it means. As I've said, I'm no scholar, so I just read them
some passages about the subject and let people make their own
decisions. If you're keeping track, then you've likely noticed that
all these folks asked to be baptized. I didn't ask them. It's not up
to me to decide what people think or feel about subjects like this.
It is a result of a pinprick of the heart and a desire to hand their
life over to Jesus.

I don't argue. I don't debate. I don't judge. I just read the
Word and let God do the rest.

When I'm talking to someone about their life and how they
live, they may have already been baptized or they may know
nothing about it. As I mentioned, Jake was baptized as an infant,
which he obviously does not remember. For that reason, it didn't

connect in any way to how he was living his life. That's why, next, I want to look at some other examples that I've found to help folks like Jake and better explain what exactly this "water plunge" might be about.

When I'm sharing the Gospel with someone, after I leave Acts 2, I usually go to Romans, where Paul was trying to help the Roman church understand what faith in Jesus really looks like. While the letter or book itself is not about baptism, Paul gave a deeper explanation on the topic. I always want people to see and read this when examining their faith. These beginnings can be very instrumental in our journey with Jesus.

You have likely noticed that I use marriage as an analogy for our commitment to Christ quite often, as did Paul. It's a relational, social, and cultural concept but also a spiritual one that people understand. If a couple is having trouble in their marriage and seeks help, the counselor will go back to where the couple began. A starting point is determined, and then you move forward to the present. That's the same approach I take in talking about the Lord. Let's figure out how or when any kind of faith started and then, *if* it went wrong, try to find solutions.

All Scripture is God-breathed and is useful for teaching, rebuking, correcting and training in righteousness. (2 Timothy 3:16)

In Romans 6:1, Paul asked a question that I've found a lot of people have been struggling with: "What shall we say, then? Shall we go on sinning so that grace may increase?"

Great question! Paul found out that the word on the street

was if you sin and mess up, the grace of God covers it, because the debt was paid when Jesus died on the cross. *Sweet!* So we can then go sin all we want, and it's covered, right?

Let's answer that question in terms of your car insurance. The company says if you pay a set amount each month to be insured, then your vehicle will be covered, no matter how much repairs cost. *Sweet!* So you could go destroy your car over and over again and insurance would keep fixing it, no matter what it costs. But if you did that, your insurance company would quickly let you know that that is definitely not the case! They can, at any point, cancel your coverage because the understanding is that you are not out *trying* to destroy your car. That's just common sense understood in the agreement.

Paul emphatically let the Romans know what he thought about people claiming to know Jesus but then sinning all they want and still expecting the grace of Jesus to cover them. His answer: "By no means! We are those who have died to sin; how can we live in it any longer?" (v. 2).

This whole idea comes back to what we read in Galatians 5 about how we live. Paul used this language in Galatians and again in Romans, explaining that how you live your life is a big deal. Next, he did something interesting—Paul made a connection to the physical act of baptism.

> Or don't you know that all of us who were baptized into Christ Jesus were baptized into his death? We were therefore buried with him through baptism into death in order that, just as Christ was raised from the dead through the glory of the Father, we too may live a new life. (Romans 6:3–4)

I love Paul's deeper dive to give way more detail about baptism. He explained exactly what happens in this act of plunging into water by tying it to the Gospel. In 1 Corinthians 15, Paul told the church that Jesus died, was buried, and was raised back to life, and baptism represents those events using water. Oftentimes, when I have a conversation with people and read these passages, they better understand the connection between baptism and Jesus' death, burial, and resurrection.

Paul explained that we don't keep sinning in the way we once lived, because we died to our old life when we were baptized. We were buried, just as Jesus was buried. We are raised, just as He was raised to a *new* life. So when we are baptized, we are reenacting what Jesus did. Those three things—death, burial, resurrection—are the keys to the Gospel. This is what Peter was telling people in Acts 2 right after Jesus left. When I share the Good News with anyone, I want them to know exactly what the Bible says, to understand exactly what they are doing and what it means.

From there, I go ahead and flip a few pages over to Romans 10:9.

> If you declare with your mouth, "Jesus is Lord," and believe in your heart that God raised him from the dead, you will be saved.

This confession of Jesus as Lord is usually where a move toward God starts. Not just a onetime declaration of this phrase but the beginning of a new lifestyle. Baptism represents the rebirth of a person spiritually. Just as a marriage is marked by an official ceremony, signing of papers, rings, vows, and a new life formed where two become one, so baptism is a symbol of surrender to Christ, the death of the old man or woman, and resurrection to a new life with God.

As I stated in the last chapter, I go into the details with people because I want them to read the Bible for themselves and make their own life choice. The person has to believe the Bible and see Scripture as essential to their lives because they will need God's Word as their journey begins in being a disciple of Jesus Christ. They will have the rest of their life to study, learn, and grow in maturity. Even if they have heard some of these things in the past, they are now reading it for themselves. But many times, it's the first time they have seen these truths in the Bible.

NEVER RUN FROM AN OPPORTUNITY

We had some friends over one night and sat out by the fire, just catching up and telling stories. A pastor we know brought a guy with him named Charlie. It was our first time to meet, so I really didn't know anything about Charlie's faith. You never know 'til you ask, right? I was telling a story about someone getting baptized when Charlie comes out with, "*I've* never been baptized."

Even though it was after midnight by then, I grabbed my Bible and read some of these passages to him. My wife had gone in the house, and as she was coming back out, I said, "Korie, go get some towels!" Over the years, she has heard that request many times. She knew exactly what that meant. Charlie had been to church and certainly believed in Jesus. Now we were walking down to my lake in the dark of night for him to get baptized. The reason? No one had ever asked him about it or explained it to him, but as soon as I began sharing stories of others getting baptized, there was something in his spirit that told him he needed to know more. Once he read the scriptures for himself, he didn't want to wait another second. After Charlie went back home, he texted me every Sunday after that night. To this day, I still have him in my phone contacts as "Charlie Get Some Towels." Every week, his texts simply say, "Happy Sunday!"

I find it interesting that in the book of Acts, most of the conversations about the Gospel didn't happen on Sunday mornings, but all throughout the week, anytime, all the time. Gospel conversations were popping up constantly, even though that was a very difficult time to be a Christian.

One of my favorite stories in the book of Acts is found in chapter 16, though it starts out sounding hopeless:

> They seized Paul and Silas and dragged them into the marketplace to face the authorities. . . . The crowd joined in the attack against Paul and Silas, and the magistrates ordered them to be stripped and beaten with rods. After they had been severely flogged, they were thrown into prison, and the jailer was commanded to guard them carefully. When he received these orders, he put them in the inner cell and fastened their feet in the stocks. (Acts 16:19, 22–24)

Paul and Silas landed in jail because of their work in the name of Jesus. But notice the details: they were stripped, beaten, thrown in a cell, and placed in stocks. Imprisonment *and* pain. But what's amazing is what they did *after* they were thrown in jail and treated so badly. They weren't yelling and screaming. They weren't threatening the people who mistreated them.

"About midnight Paul and Silas were praying and singing hymns to God, and the other prisoners were listening to them." (v. 25)

Notice what they were doing: praying and singing. The time? Midnight. The other prisoners' response? Listening to them. I'm sure Paul and Silas were the only two guys being positive in these circumstances. People are always listening and paying attention to how we live. Because of that, you never know when the opportunity will open up to change someone's life. That's exactly what was about to happen in this lonely jail cell:

Suddenly there was such a violent earthquake that the foundations of the prison were shaken. At once all the prison doors flew open, and everyone's chains came loose. The jailer woke up, and when he saw the prison doors open, he drew his sword and was about to kill himself because he thought the prisoners had escaped. But Paul shouted, "Don't harm yourself! We are all here!" (vv. 26–28)

I have to admit, I would have totally misread this sign and miracle from God. I would have left the jail immediately, thinking He had provided a way out for me and my friend when the doors flew open and the chains dropped. I would have thought God made this situation right because I had been faithful to Him. I would have thought that the jailer deserved a terrible fate because of all the injustice he had carried out. I would have forgotten that this was not about *me* but about *others*. I would have forgotten that Jesus forgave others, even the ones who nailed Him to a cross.

But Paul didn't forget. Paul didn't run. He saw a great opportunity. He knew that everyone had noticed how he reacted to the punishment that was not warranted. He knew how strange it must have looked and sounded that he and Silas were praising God in their suffering. He probably realized that this moment would matter; that at the very time he could have left, he stayed. He knew this was about *others*. He knew that to be a Gospeler, there is another step we have to take—to let people know *why* we act the way we do.

Check this out:

> The jailer called for lights, rushed in and fell trembling before Paul and Silas. He then brought them out and asked, "Sirs, what must I do to be saved?" They replied, "Believe in the Lord Jesus, and you will be saved—you and your household." Then they spoke the word of the Lord to him and to all the others in his house. (vv. 29–32)

Because Paul and Silas had shown everyone in that jail what it looked like to follow Jesus, the jailer's heart was opened. The jailer had the same reaction those folks in Acts 2 did. He asked, "What must I do to be saved?" Paul and Silas had shown the Gospel not with words but with actions. Both men came to the same conclusion: God had orchestrated this moment so that someone could hear the Gospel and be saved.

"Believe in the Lord Jesus" was the answer. Paul wanted this jailer to know the *why* of what he'd just witnessed. It wasn't that they were special or supernatural people, but there was something else that separated them—Jesus. Then "they spoke the word of the Lord to him and to all the others in his house" (v. 32). At this late hour of the night, in this strange circumstance, around the time the officials would be finding out what the heck was going on at the jail, after all the townspeople had attacked them for preaching Jesus—that was the moment they took the time to sit and speak the word of the Lord. Like I said before— one mission, one message.

This is where I think, all too often, we simply fall short in sharing the Gospel. If it had been us in the jail with that guy, we may have misread the blessing and said nothing at all, or just said "Believe in Jesus" and left it at that. We may not have taken the time to speak truth and read the Word with him. But Paul and Silas did just that. Everything else stopped because sharing the Gospel with the jailer and his family was that important.

I'm sure Paul constantly remembered what his life looked like prior to seeing Jesus on the road to Damascus and then being blind for three days before his own baptism (Acts 9). I'm sure experiencing all that would make anyone stop and reflect on the importance of deciding to live their life for the Lord. Paul was not going to let another second go by without giving this man the same opportunity Jesus had given him.

So watch what happened next.

At that hour of the night the jailer took them and washed their wounds; then immediately he and all his household were bap- tized. The jailer brought them into his house and set a meal before them; he was filled with joy because he had come to believe in God—he and his whole household. (16:33–34)

These verses tell us why Paul and Silas thought it was important to go to that level of sacrifice and obedience in the middle of the night. I might have just said, "Look, we really have to get out of here!" But they didn't. They were committed to see this all the way through. The fact that this was so important to Paul and Silas tells me that it should be important to me too. I know it was important to that jailer and his family. And this is exactly what constantly reminds me that it's important to wade into freezing water in a nasty cow pond or get out my Bible to talk to a new friend even if it's after midnight. It's not about me.

Now I want to apply this to your life and ask, Are you having these middle-of-the-night Bible discussions with others?

Are there situations that come up during the week where you are speaking the Word of the Lord to folks?

If your answer is rarely or never, then take the time to read through the book of Acts to see how these people were living. The more you speak the name of Jesus, the more you will begin having more and more stories that end like this. They will happen all throughout your week. I believe the opportunities are already there, and God is ready to show you.

ANYWHERE, ANYTIME

As you've likely already figured out, most of my stories of talking to others about Jesus don't happen on Sunday mornings. When I go to a church building, it's usually with a bunch of people who already profess to know and live for Jesus. So I sing and listen to someone give a lesson from the Bible. I may talk with some people before or after the service, but rarely do many of us ever encounter someone there who is asking about how they can actually get in on the Gospel.

Let's return to my Jake story.

After the cow pond dunking, I headed back to my friend's hunting camp. What I haven't mentioned yet is that my camera guy at the time was with me. I usually have someone go hunting with me who can capture the experience on video, so he and I had been hunting together before Jake came back out to get baptized. He's normally videoing wildlife, but once the baptism started, that quickly became his focus. Driving back, he said, "I don't really understand what I just saw." That's when I realized the story wasn't over; it was just beginning. So I started talking with him, gathering his story and sharing the Word.

As we pulled up to the camp, he professed that he, too, was ready for Jesus and also wanted to get baptized. I explained that we could do something similar to the cow pond, or maybe somewhere inside would be a bit more comfortable. He wisely chose the indoor route after seeing Jake run to the truck after emerging from the sludgy water a bright cherry red.

Soon, all the guys at the deer camp found out about Jake and then were even more fired up to find out that one more guy was ready to go too. We all gathered for prayer and decided that we would attempt the baptism in a bathtub. Thank goodness, my buddy just happened to have an oversized tub.

Now, bathtub baptisms can be tricky. Kind of like with frying a turkey, you need to be careful with how much liquid you put in the pot before you drop in the bird! In a bathroom packed with all the guys, we eyeballed the water level and he got in the tub. Most knew exactly what was happening, but a few were like those prisoners listening to Paul and Silas singing and praying in that ol' jail cell; they didn't really understand what they were witnessing. Soon, my camera guy took the plunge just like Jake had. On a weeknight. Not at a church. In a bathtub. In a bathroom full of deer hunters. All after seeing someone else "hear the word of the Lord" and take action by "believing in the Lord Jesus," just like in Acts 16 with the jailer and his family.

CART BEFORE THE HORSE

Often, when I am gathering someone's story like Jake's, they may have been baptized in the past, especially when they were younger. Many people have experiences like that when they were a child or teenager. Some seem to be fruitful, while others are more like some kind of awards ceremony where the grandparents come and pictures are taken, but to the child, these events are soon forgotten and not life-changing. I also talk to much older people who came to the Lord and were baptized but felt they didn't really grasp exactly what they were doing, and since then their lives have in no way been a witness to the new life that Scripture says is found in Jesus.

This can be confusing to folks, for sure, especially when it leads to a life that ends up in a sin cellar, has in no way looked Christlike, and has yielded little to no "fruit of the Spirit" but instead looks more like "the acts of the sinful nature." As a Gospeler, I can't take the easy path and say, "I'm not sure what to make of that. . . . Well, good luck!" I want to help them walk through their life and see if the Word can shed some light.

Acts 19 is one conversation that helps some people find clarity:

> While Apollos was at Corinth, Paul took the road through the interior and arrived at Ephesus. There he found some disciples and asked them, "Did you receive the Holy Spirit when you believed?" They answered, "No, we have not even heard that there is a Holy Spirit." So Paul asked, "Then what baptism did you receive?" "John's baptism," they replied. Paul said, "John's baptism was a baptism of repentance. He told the people to believe in the one coming after him, that is, in Jesus." (vv. 1–4)

Take notice of the first thing Paul did, which hopefully you are seeing is a clear theme for a Gospeler: he asked a question. Here, that was, "Did you receive the Holy Spirit when you believed?" Perhaps something they had done or said made Paul think they did not have the Holy Spirit, but regardless of why he asked, he got a response that proved the need for his question: "No, we have not even heard that there is a Holy Spirit." Next, he asked specifically about baptism.

Paul then clarified John's baptism, but most importantly, he wanted them to know the main focus—Jesus. He also wanted them to know John was all about Jesus and that, while they may have indeed repented of their sins, none of it was worth anything without Jesus.

So what was their response? "On hearing this, they were baptized in the name of the Lord Jesus" (v. 5).

Now that they understood *who* it was actually about, they were baptized again. This is helpful when talking to folks who

> ANY BAPTISM THAT OCCURS WITHOUT JESUS IS JUST A TEMPORARY EVENT. WITH JESUS, IT'S AN ETERNAL EXPERIENCE.

may have a similar story with a previous baptism. Paul could have just told them how it all worked, right? He could have let them know about Jesus and the Holy Spirit. But he went all the way and simply baptized them again. Any baptism that occurs without Jesus is just a temporary event. With Jesus, it's an eternal experience.

Toward the end of the New Testament, we find a couple of letters (books) written by Peter. Remember, in Acts, he had initially told people to be baptized after Jesus' resurrection. In his first letter, Peter spoke of baptism in a different way.

And this water symbolizes baptism that now saves you also— not the removal of dirt from the body but the pledge of a clear conscience toward God. It saves you by the resurrection of Jesus Christ. (1 Peter 3:21)

Peter described baptism as a clearing of our conscience toward God. I find that many people I meet and share with are looking for just that—a clear conscience. They are wandering through life wanting to be right with God but aren't sure if they actually are. They are uncertain of how to live their life. This type of person rarely shares the Good News with others because they are not sure who they are themselves. Like Paul helped the people from Ephesus realize, they may not even have the Holy Spirit. That could be the real problem in the first place. They may be trying to fight the battle of life without the very Helper God has sent to allow them to walk in victory.

Jesus not only came to help people escape the sin cellar and take away their shame and regrets of the past, but He said the Spirit was coming after Him to live in His people from that moment forward (John 14:26–27). That is the very picture we experience in the symbolism of baptism when salvation becomes the game changer for how we live.

Don't you know that you yourselves are God's temple and that God's Spirit dwells in your midst? (1 Corinthians 3:16)

Eight

INTERSTELLAR

INTERSTELLAR, THE 2014 HIT FILM ABOUT SPACE TRAVEL, PLACED THIS word firmly into our mainstream culture. To be interstellar is to be "located, taking place, or traveling among the stars."[1] For believers in Jesus, looking to the skies reminds us of heavenly things. As we see throughout the book of Acts, the Holy Spirit is the connection between God and His people—the One who causes up there to take place down here, to make God's will "on earth as it is in heaven" (Matthew 6:10). He steps down to where we are so that He can then invite us upward to where He is.

> HE STEPS DOWN TO WHERE WE ARE SO THAT HE CAN THEN INVITE US UPWARD TO WHERE HE IS.

In so many people's stories that I have been a part of, I've gotten to experience God stepping into people's worlds and inviting them upward. Take Jake, for example. Just when I thought his story was wrapped up, it turned out there was more to come.

After Jake's salvation, he was fired up. My buddy Adam, who

set up our original conversation, told me that Jake met with his brother to talk as soon as possible. Before long, his brother came to Jesus and was baptized too. Next, Jake desperately wanted to share the Gospel with his father. All this reminded me a lot of Paul and Silas's jailer, who wanted his whole family to be part of his spiritual journey.

That's when Jake reached out to me. I was going to be speaking at an event in Kansas City soon, so we set up a meeting at an apartment there. He was going to bring someone else for me to speak with. This would be a one-night, one-shot deal. Jake had warned me that his guy was, well, let's just say, rough around the edges. When I arrived, I saw that a few other guys were there also. After some small talk, I began asking questions to get to know his dad's story, like I always do.

He talked about a faith journey that started at the age of nine, to which I asked the obvious question: "Okay, so how's it been since then?" From all he went on to tell me, not so good. He didn't even mention the name of Jesus in his story. His life now consisted of one-night stands with women, "trying them out" in hopes of finding another wife.

His path was really dark, and he had a strong sense of pride and arrogance mixed with many of the things from Paul's list of sins in Galatians 5. As I read the passage to him, I could see he was trying to come to grips with the move he had made toward God as a kid versus the life he was currently living that seemed very selfish and worldly.

Yet, as always, if he felt like he was right with God, then I wasn't going to argue with him. It was his decision, not mine. But I know the Gospel has the power to move people in these moments. Even though he acted as if he was interested in being baptized that night, I sensed he was not ready to go all in. Something stirring inside made me press him more about what this meant. He was not very convincing that he would give up pursuing women in the way he had been. He told me he was even flying in women from other places. In fact, he probably already had dates set up for that week, having had no idea we would be sitting around talking about God on that night.

I knew if he made his decision that night, he would have to start tearing down the lifestyle he had been building for years when the next day came. I knew it would be a huge challenge for him to truly change and repent. I could see it in his eyes and on his face. His lifestyle reeked of sin. He would have to make big changes—changes the people around him might not understand or be happy about. In situations like this, it's very easy to second-guess any decision to change your life, so it's important to be sure.

In the middle of all this, I was thinking to myself, *I can't in good conscience baptize this guy.* That was rare for me, because it's so hard to know someone's heart. But on this particular night, I really wasn't sure about this man, and I never want to cheapen the Gospel just to be able to talk someone into a decision. Christ requires 100 percent of our lives. The person must be ready to go all in. As we talked about in the previous chapter, there has to be that "What must I do?" moment.

As the other guys were talking to him, I just closed my eyes and silently prayed, *God, I'm not sure about this guy. Please give me something to tell him.* I heard an inner voice say, "Read him Luke 14." I knew exactly what that meant and what I needed to show him. Luke 14:25–33 is the story of Jesus telling a crowd about the cost of being His disciple.

Large crowds were traveling with Jesus, and he turned and said to them, "If anyone comes to me but loves his father, mother, wife, children, brothers, or sisters—or even life—more than me, he cannot be my follower. Whoever is not willing to carry his cross and follow me cannot be my follower. If you want to build a tower, you first sit down and decide how much it will cost, to see if you have enough money to finish the job. If you don't, you might lay the foundation, but you would not be able to finish. Then all who would see it would make fun of you, saying, 'This person began to build but was not able to finish.'

"If a king is going to fight another king, first he will sit down and plan. He will decide if he and his ten thousand soldiers can defeat the other king who has twenty thousand soldiers. If he can't, then while the other king is still far away, he will send some people to speak to him and ask for peace. In the same way, you must give up everything you have to be my follower." (NCV)

After I read him the whole passage, I asked point-blank, "Are you going to give up this thing you're doing with women?" He paused to think. I had no idea what he was going to say. But he looked up at me and said, "Yes, I'm ready." So after a little prep work, we all gathered around a small tub in the apartment bathroom, and I baptized him.

First John 1:5–2:2 talks about how we need to turn the tables on our sin and get serious once we "claim to have fellowship with him."

This is the message we have heard from him and declare to you: God is light; in him there is no darkness at all. If we claim to have fellowship with him and yet walk in the darkness, we lie and do not live out the truth. But if we walk in the light, as he is in the light, we have fellowship with one another, and the blood of Jesus, his Son, purifies us from all sin.

If we claim to be without sin, we deceive ourselves and the truth is not in us. If we confess our sins, he is faithful and just and will forgive us our sins and purify us from all unrighteousness. If we claim we have not sinned, we make him out to be a liar and his word is not in us. My dear children, I write this to you so that you will not sin. But if anybody does sin, we have an advocate with the Father—Jesus Christ, the Righteous One. He is the atoning sacrifice for our sins, and not only for ours but also for the sins of the whole world.

I always like to read this passage to anyone who has crossed that line of faith because it speaks of walking in the light, not darkness, and we are also reminded who provided the light—Jesus. It also tells us who covers us when we do sin. Jesus has forgiven our past and is still advocating for us in the future.

GOSPELERS ASK QUESTIONS, SHARE THE GOOD NEWS, AND WATCH IT SPREAD EVEN FURTHER.

For Jake, what started as a conversation in a pickup truck months earlier had now led us to another person coming to faith. Gospelers ask questions, share the Good News, and watch it spread even further. Two thousand years after Jesus, halfway around the planet from where He lived, the Gospel is still showing its power to people. Just as the Lord said so many times, "Whoever has ears, let them hear."

FATHER, SON, AND *WHO?*

So what exactly was that inner voice I was hearing when I was praying and asking what to do about Jake's dad? Who is this Holy Spirit? As I've told you about my many conversations with people, I have mentioned this third person of the Trinity. Once someone has committed to Jesus, there is an important thing God thought of to help His people live the life worthy of being called His disciples: He put His Spirit in us.

For everyone coming out of a sinful past, there is definitely a need for the Holy Spirit to help. God didn't just task us with following Him and then leave us alone. To repeat John 14:26, Jesus said, "But the Advocate, the Holy Spirit, whom the Father will send in my name, will teach you all things and will remind you of everything I have said to you." The Holy Spirit will also create our ability and opportunity to witness for Him.

Depending on your church background, you likely know that the Holy Spirit is perhaps the most misunderstood person of the Trinity. Some folks *rarely* talk about Him, while others seem to *constantly* talk about Him. In some churches, He seems to be nonexistent, and in others, He's the star of the show. Because of this difference, I am in no way going to tackle all the many trains of thought on this topic. In fact, when I'm talking to people about starting this journey, I keep it simple. I let them read and discover more about the Holy Spirit living in them.

Going back to my launch point where I usually start a conversation—Galatians 5—we read that the Spirit's work will yield the fruit of love, joy, peace, patience, kindness, goodness, faithfulness, gentleness, and self-control. The way we know we have the Holy Spirit in our lives is that we produce these kinds

WHEN GOD LIVES
IN US, WE BECOME
DIFFERENT.

of fruit. This also ties back to Acts chapter 2, where Peter said we will receive the gift of the Holy Spirit.

The whole idea is that when God lives in us, we become *different*. This concept should not be foreign to us. We have seen normal, good folks who get hooked on drugs and turn into very different people. We have all heard of killers who commit horrific crimes because they have some dark evil inside that drives them. If we can understand that bad things live in us, then we can also understand the concept of God's Spirit living in people. At the basic level, the Spirit produces good in our lives. We find ourselves doing good even when we may not feel like it, because that's the Spirit being active in our lives.

In chapter 4, we looked at a conversation Jesus had with a woman at a well who was *not* very religious (John 4). But right before that in Scripture, in John 3, Jesus had another interesting exchange with a member of the Jewish ruling council who was *super* religious. These two very different people had really similar questions.

As we look at this late-night conversation, watch for Jesus talking about the Spirit:

Now there was a Pharisee, a man named Nicodemus who was a member of the Jewish ruling council. He came to Jesus at night and said, "Rabbi, we know that you are a teacher who has come from God. For no one could perform the signs you are doing if God were not with him." Jesus replied, "Very truly I tell you, no one can see the kingdom of God unless they are born again."

"How can someone be born when they are old?" Nicodemus asked. "Surely they cannot enter a second time into their mother's womb to be born!"

Jesus answered, "Very truly I tell you, no one can enter the kingdom of God unless they are born of water and the Spirit. Flesh gives birth to flesh, but the Spirit gives birth to spirit. You should not be surprised at my saying, 'You must be born again.' The wind blows wherever it pleases. You hear its sound, but you cannot tell where it comes from or where it is going. So it is with everyone born of the Spirit."

"How can this be?" Nicodemus asked. (vv. 1–9)

Who better to explain the Good News than Jesus! Even though the whole Gospel had not played out yet, He was telling this guy that people would have to be reborn through a combination of water and the Spirit. Nicodemus was utterly confused, as we all probably would be. I remind most church folks that we can't expect people who have never really read the Bible to know all it has to say. These things need to be explained, just like anything else in life. (And Nicodemus didn't have the luxury of searching YouTube like we do.)

This conversation with Jesus is so important to all of us who try to explain what it means to follow Him. Nicodemus appeared to understand that Jesus was God. While that had gotten his attention, he did not understand how he could become a part of it all. People may see our lives as believers and wonder how they could be a part of this movement we call Christianity as well. But we can't just expect them to figure it all out on their own. Walking them through how to be born again takes time and patience. Jesus explained that same concept to Nicodemus.

"You are Israel's teacher," said Jesus, "and do you not understand these things? Very truly I tell you, we speak of what we know, and we testify to what we have seen, but still you people do not accept our testimony. I have spoken to you of earthly things and you do not believe; how then will you believe if I speak of heavenly things? No one has ever gone into heaven except the one who came from heaven—the Son of Man. Just as Moses lifted up the snake in the wilderness, so the Son of Man must be lifted up, that everyone who believes may have eternal life in him." (vv. 10–15)

Jesus told him these were "heavenly things," beyond what can be seen. Of course, there are some people at this point who will say, "That's where you lost me. I'm out." If they simply choose not to believe, then they will miss this very important Helper in their life. When you get to the Holy Spirit in conversation, that's going to require the person to have some faith, because it won't make sense until you *are* "born again," which is exactly what Jesus was telling Nicodemus.

DARKNESS TO LIGHT, DEATH TO LIFE

Korie and I are blessed to have beautiful grandbabies. One day when we were talking about pregnancy and childbirth, she shared a spiritual analogy she had realized. Korie said that when a baby is born, it must feel like death to him or her. Now before you say, like I did, "Wait . . . what?" I'll tell you what she explained to me. When you are a baby in your mother's womb, you have everything you need—food, warmth, and comfort. And then suddenly, one day, you start to move. It's not an easy experience; it's actually pretty painful from what I understand. Then, in a few minutes or hours, you are squeezed out; you move out of the only place and life you have ever known! You have no idea where you are, but it does not feel at all like where you are meant to be. It's bright. It's cold. You feel pain. You feel discomfort. So you scream! But as you scream, everyone is really excited—except you! You probably think in your little baby brain, *I must have just died!* But instead, you were born; you entered into a new life. In that moment, what we call "life" makes no sense. But over time, as you begin to grow and learn, it all starts to connect. Korie was explaining that she thinks death is like another birth for believers—a birth into the eternal life we were made for. I had never thought of it that way!

When Jesus told Nicodemus that we all must be born again, He meant the old self must die, and we must be made new. Even Jesus, because He had come to earth and was fully God but was also fully man, was going to die and be made new. As a new creation, you will have the Spirit of God living inside of you. Coming from beyond this world, it's interstellar. A new life that is not earthbound but of a different dimension. One just as real as where we are currently living.

Let's continue with Jesus' conversation with Nicodemus in John 3:

> "For God so loved the world that he gave his one and only Son,
> that whoever believes in him shall not perish but have eternal
> life. For God did not send his Son into the world to condemn

the world, but to save the world through him. Whoever believes in him is not condemned, but whoever does not believe stands condemned already because they have not believed in the name of God's one and only Son." (vv. 16–18)

Jesus explained the *why* to this religious leader. God did all this because He loves us. His love is the reason Jesus was talking to Nicodemus. This may not make any sense from a worldly viewpoint, but it does from a heavenly perspective.

"This is the verdict: Light has come into the world, but people loved darkness instead of light because their deeds were evil. Everyone who does evil hates the light, and will not come into the light for fear that their deeds will be exposed. But whoever lives by the truth comes into the light, so that it may be seen plainly that what they have done has been done in the sight of God." (vv. 19–21)

Jesus went back to *how* we live our earthly lives. This is the same message that Peter, Paul, John, and everyone else focused on later as well. Light versus darkness. When a baby is born into this world, he or she doesn't even realize that their life before was in darkness. That is, until the light comes.

For us, we see the darkness all around. It's not new; it's been the same since the fall in the garden of Eden. But now the Gospel offers us a choice—live in the light or stay in the darkness.

The Holy Spirit of God helps us along the way as we walk in the light. In verse 8, Jesus compared Him to the wind. I'm not sure exactly how wind works, but I can certainly feel it, even though I can't see it. The Holy Spirit is the part of God that is on the earth today, inside of those who believe, transforming our spirits and making us more and more holy.

Here's another passage from Jesus to explain about the Holy Spirit:

> "If you love me, keep my commands. And I will ask the Father,
> and he will give you another advocate to help you and be with
> you forever—the Spirit of truth. The world cannot accept him,
> because it neither sees him nor knows him. But you know him,
> for he lives with you and will be in you." (John 14:15–17)

The Holy Spirit is the big difference between those who follow Jesus and those who don't believe. He lives *in* us. It's not the good *in us* that pours out to others but rather the good *of Him* that comes out of our lives. We are still broken and sinful people, but now, saved by the grace of Jesus, we are full of a new Spirit—the Holy Spirit.

> IT'S NOT THE GOOD *IN US* THAT POURS OUT TO OTHERS BUT RATHER THE GOOD *OF HIM* THAT COMES OUT OF OUR LIVES.

In Romans 5, Paul talked about what the Holy Spirit will produce in our lives:

> Therefore, since we have been justified by faith, we have
> peace with God through our Lord Jesus Christ. Through him
> we have also obtained access by faith into this grace in which
> we stand, and we rejoice in hope of the glory of God. Not only
> that, but we rejoice in our sufferings, knowing that suffering
> produces endurance, and endurance produces character, and
> character produces hope, and hope does not put us to shame,

because God's love has been poured into our hearts through the Holy Spirit who has been given to us. (vv. 1–5 ESV)

Korie and I have been together for thirty-plus years of marriage. For all that time, we have always sought peace with each other. It's not easy, but that peace leads to endurance. When we first got married we had no idea what we were doing, but because of our commitment to the Lord and each other, the trials didn't destroy us; they strengthened us—much like what Paul was trying to tell the church in Rome as he talked about endurance.

The peace from God that comes through Jesus is so similar to marriage. We have sufferings that produce endurance, which builds character that leads to hope—all produced by God's love, which was poured into us through the Holy Spirit. Over time, Korie and I started to know what the other was going to say. We would hear something and know what each of us would think about it. This melded our own spirits together, just like the Holy Spirit who lives in us.

There's another hope that should help us here on earth and motivate us even more to share with other people as we live as followers of Jesus. Another interstellar gift—the idea of living together beyond this life. The hope of eternal life, as my father says, "is the only plan I've ever heard for getting off of this planet alive," so he's sticking with it. So am I.

SEEING THE UNSEEN

One of the tricks I came to understand early on in business is being able to forecast—to have foresight to foresee things *before* they happen. If you wait until it's obvious to everyone, the opportunity may be gone. Those who see things first are usually rewarded, and some have been wildly successful. We see that on almost every episode of *Shark Tank*.

I had some baby versions of this happen early in my business career when I was a young, newly hired leader of our family business, Duck Commander. Dad and I were partners, so we always had to go over the ideas I was bringing to the table. He wasn't exactly business savvy, so he mostly yielded to what I thought was best. But there were a few times he took exception.

The first was a product change. We had been producing and releasing our hunts on VHS tapes and, before long, had sold thousands all over the world. But I had been exposed to this new media coming along called digital video discs, or DVDs. For many reasons, they were much better. They didn't wear out, and you didn't have to rewind them. I made the official call to not release our hunts on VHS tapes anymore. We would switch to DVDs from then on.

Well, Dad didn't think this was a good idea. He could not believe I was not going to have VHS tapes available to our customers. "I have a VHS player at my house!" he said louder than was necessary. I told him I realized that, but soon, he would probably be one of the last people in the state to still watch those. Even with that speed bump, it was the right move. Not too difficult to predict that one.

The next paradigm shift was the World Wide Web. Dad thought it was crazy when I wanted a company website. I tried to tell him I thought people would be buying items off the internet in the future. I remember him saying, "Well, you tell people if they want a Duck Commander duck call, they can pick up the phone and call!" I let him know a few times that a website was definitely where business was heading. To be fair, I bit my tongue when my team suggested we sell on Amazon, but they were right.

Just like there's an ability to foresee trends in business, there's the interstellar aspect of faith too.

So we fix our eyes not on what is seen, but on what is unseen, since what is seen is temporary, but what is unseen is eternal. (2 Corinthians 4:18)

An unseen Holy Spirit. An unseen heaven. For us today, an unseen Jesus. We only have stories passed down from those who claimed they did see Him. Those who claimed He was sent by an unseen God. That's one of the toughest parts of why the job of the Gospeler is not easy. Our changed lives may be the only representation that people *do* see. That's the very reason that the way we live our lives is such an important testimony. People can *see* the fruit of the Spirit by how we live. They can *see* Jesus in how we treat others. They can *see* God by how we live for Him. Before we even open our mouths, all the goodness of God can be seen living in us.

Paul explained that responsibility in 2 Corinthians 5:20:

We are therefore Christ's ambassadors, as though God were making his appeal through us. We implore you on Christ's behalf: Be reconciled to God.

Just by the simple fact that we *want* to share with others, God's Spirit is shown. What other reason would we possibly have to care about people's problems and want to offer them answers?

While I was writing this book, I talked to Jake about his life and how his walk with the Lord is going. There is always a connection and a bond with folks when you help them find their way to the Gospel. In that conversation, he told me something I didn't know about that cold day in the cow pond.

Jake said what impressed on him the most was the fact that I was so focused on his life that day. This was in 2013, when our show was one of the biggest on TV. I had just flown in from New York where we had been on a float in the Macy's Thanksgiving Day Parade. Then, the very next day, I was sitting in that men's Bible study in Kansas where I met him.

As Jake reminded me of the story, I had forgotten all those details. He couldn't believe that I was not talking about being on national TV, telling me, "You only seemed to care about where *I* was with the Lord. All of the things you had going on at the time didn't seem to matter to you."

I have told Jake's story many, many times to people, yet rarely do I think to bring up the Macy's parade. The reason is because true life change happened for this man that ultimately affected his wife, son, brother, and dad, and it still resonates with others he talks to today, which is far more important both now and in eternity than a parade in New York City.

I get encouraged when I hear how, once the Spirit of God is embraced, He moves in new places. When most of the other stuff in life is just quickly forgotten, sharing Jesus with people lasts. When my life is over, I hope it's the main thing that is remembered about me.

ONLY PASSING THROUGH

A friend of mine named Rick called me late one night. Through tears, he told me he had been diagnosed with pancreatic cancer. I knew enough to know this was really bad. We talked for hours about life, his kids, and the future. In situations like that, it's always hard to find the right words. As I've said, when I tell people about the Gospel, I usually share 1 Corinthians 15, which explains the resurrection of Christ and what He did for us. That night with Rick, I went to the end of the chapter where it says,

> "Death has been swallowed up in victory." "Where, O death, is your victory? Where, O death, is your sting?" The sting of death is sin, and the power of sin is the law. But thanks be to God! He gives us the victory through our Lord Jesus Christ. (vv. 54–57)

I read this passage to give him comfort. When I was done, Rick asked if I would baptize him. Obviously, I agreed. We had spent so much time together in the past and didn't realize that time was about to be cut short. At this point in Rick's life, he held nothing back about his belief and hope in the Gospel as his focus was moving away from this life to the next.

He came down to Louisiana and, in front of many people, obeyed the Gospel through baptism. There were lots of tears. When you know you may not have long to live on this earth, every moment is more special. In reality, none of us knows how long we have.

Rick would go on to be with the Lord shortly after his baptism at the age of forty-six.

We all struggle with being focused on ourselves. That's why I think I would be super self-focused if I believed this life is all I have. That's also why we're not surprised when we see so many people today being self-absorbed, because they do think this is all there is.

But we will all move on from this earth. We are not here long at all. Only passing through. The Gospel is Good News while we are here on the earth, but it's even better news for living beyond this life. Knowing we are secure about eternity can and should change how we live. Heaven gives us hope and a greater meaning when bad things happen here. I can't imagine living life with no hope of what is beyond.

For the believer, the interstellar awaits. We're like we all were when we were babies in the womb, living in the comforts of darkness, not realizing that the light doesn't bring death at all, but real life instead.

"Very truly I tell you, whoever hears my word and believes him who sent me has eternal life and will not be judged but has crossed over from death to life." (John 5:24)

Nine

RETAILER

MY FIRST BUSINESS VENTURE WAS WHEN I WAS NINE YEARS OLD. I started a worm farm. Dad had an old wooden boat he had built that wouldn't float anymore. Deciding that would be the perfect place to hold my worms, I put it on two sawhorses up off the ground. Dad told me he thought that cow manure would be great to mix in with the dirt. About a mile up the road we lived on, there was a pasture with cattle. One wheelbarrow at a time, I went the mile there, shoveled in the poop, and pushed that heavy, stinky thing back until I had finished my first real moneymaker.

The next step in my business was acquiring the worms. This part was actually super fun. To this day, I pride myself on being able to find good earthworms. You have to gently pull back fallen dead leaves, looking for the right type of worm dirt that they leave behind. When they're uncovered, some take off and can crawl surprisingly fast.

I was constantly carrying around an old can for those times when the worms were really close to the surface. The perfect time is after a good rain. When the ground gets dry, they go deeper into the dirt, which, of course, makes them harder to find. But too much water is not good. It's also not good for them when the ground is cold. That happens to match up with when the fish are biting. Well, ain't that convenient for a worm business, huh?

On Saturday mornings I would sit in a chair by our boat dock with a sign that read, "Willie's Worms—5 cents apiece." Granny owned the dock, and she put an old mailbox beside it with "1 dollar" painted on the side so people could pay when they pulled up. When I was young, I always thought she had the *big* business because she didn't have to sit outside in a chair all morning. People would just put their dollar bills in the mailbox to use her dock. Alongside Granny, "Willie's Worms" made decent money; not a bad gig for a fourth grader.

As a kid, I fell in love with business. The fact that I could work hard to make my own money and not have to depend on others was very gratifying to me. Money wasn't easy to come by in those days from Mom and Dad. But with worms being a seasonal business, I knew if I wanted to keep cash coming in, I'd need to find other ways of making an income.

Fifth grade was a real turning point for my business ventures. The biggest market was at Pinecrest, the small country school where we were all trapped eight hours a day, with not much around. The nearest store was many miles away, so I had to find the right product to move to the other kids. Most of their parents sent money with them to school for the concession stand. I knew that was my opportunity.

That same year, a guy came to our house one day to buy some duck calls. He was a candy distributor and gave Dad a box of Hubba Bubba gum to give to us boys. Well, that gum got handed to me to "distribute." I'm sure that meant for me *and* my brothers, but I had a different idea. This would be my launch into a giant retail operation I ran throughout most of my fifth-grade year.

On the first day, before I even got to school, I sold a bunch of pieces of gum on the bus and knew I was onto something big! Fifty cents a piece was the price. I sold that first box quickly. Then, like any decent entrepreneur, I reinvested all my money to buy more. "Willie's Gum and Candy" was absolutely killing it! Soon, my selection grew and was far superior to the ho-hum products at the school concession stand. This beat selling worms, for sure!

But for anyone who gets a corner on the market, competition soon shows up. The Yount boys who lived up the road tried moving in on my business. Just one problem—they weren't exactly the best salesmen. Gum was my staple, with new flavors coming in all the time. I was listening to my customers' demands, and the money just kept coming. My teacher called me "The Little Tycoon." Life could not be going better. That is, until the day I got called to the principal's office.

PRINCIPAL: "Willie, are you selling gum and candy out of your locker?"

ME: "Yes sir . . . actually doin' really good." I flashed my winning sales grin.

I wondered if he was going to give me an award for entrepreneurship or innovation. I could teach other kids what to do. I could offer training sessions. Heck, I could do a talk to the entire student body on "How to Run a Small Business." At that point, I would have considered buying an ad in the yearbook. If the principal was on board, this could be a great partnership!

To my surprise, that is not at all what happened.

PRINCIPAL: "Well, the concessions workers are telling me their sales are down. Willie, I'm going to have to shut your business down. No more selling gum and candy at school."

He was stern, and I could tell he wasn't going to budge. Just like that, my whole business went kaput! "Willie's Gum and Candy" was closed with a cease-and-desist order.

Some twenty years later, when Dad thought I should be the one to take over our family business, he actually brought up the fact that I almost single-handedly shut down the school concession stand. Since I was young, I certainly had a knack for selling things. Up for the challenge, I became the head of Duck Commander.

I always thought selling duck calls was a real challenge because it's such a specific device. There didn't seem to be enough market to sell a bunch of them. But, fortunately, I was wrong. Just like that box of Hubba Bubba, a big ol' hit TV show proved that people all over the world would want one of those quackers. I bet we've sold more duck calls than anyone in history.

CUSTOMER ACQUISITION

In the kingdom of God, we all bring a unique set of skills to the table. Whether or not it's sales, the same things that make us good at our jobs or what we love to do can be used for an eternal purpose that is far more fulfilling and satisfying than just making money. We often do things at work because we have to, but we do things for God because we want to, because we need to. Like Jesus told Peter, "Now, we fish for people." He took what Peter did at work and applied it to a higher purpose.

I have found over the years that Gospelers are all different types of people. Some have been successful in business or other areas and some have not been successful at all. There are wealthy people and folks who have very little who share their faith all the same. Some never stepped into a church until halfway through their lives, while others grew up going to church every week. But all of them are determined to help others find a new meaning and purpose.

While I am staying in the lane of winning souls in this book, I also know there are many other ways Christians can use their talents for God. Some examples are disciplers, nursery workers, serving teams, counselors, prayer warriors, community helpers, doctors, nurses, pilots, and technical teams. The list goes on and on. The church is made up of so many people, all with numerous useful skills. But I do believe the calling is on *everyone* to spread the Gospel to others. As we talked about in chapter 8, Paul said in 2 Corinthians 5:20, "We are therefore Christ's ambassadors, as though God were making his appeal through us."

My goal in these pages is to deal with the frontline work of getting "new customers," to use business language. Of course, it's not only about new customers. There are many other departments that are vitally important. But if you stop having any new folks find you, you can start the clock on when your business will eventually die off.

Let's apply that thought to our faith: if there were no new converts to Jesus from this moment on, Christianity would be gone in a few decades. But that's what is so crazy. It *never* died out, but grew—from its very beginning when Jesus was here, then throughout the book of Acts. The Good News of Jesus exploded.

So *how* and *why* did it keep going? I believe the better question is, *Who* kept it going? God has to be the reason. Nothing has ever kept going like this Jesus movement. Many people

> IF THERE WERE NO NEW CONVERTS TO JESUS FROM THIS MOMENT ON, CHRISTIANITY WOULD BE GONE IN A FEW DECADES.

saw Him *alive* after they watched Him *die*. There's nothing special about us as Christians that could keep something like this going for over two thousand years! It's not us; it's who lives in us. It's not for our purpose; it's for God's purpose.

In fact, as believers, we have done more in our history that certainly should have stopped this movement in its tracks. If we tried to list all the damage that folks have done to others in the name of Christianity, the list would be too long. Thank God that for us all, the message is still being spread around the globe.

So let's look at where we are today. Now, I'm not a big stats guy. In fact, I don't think I ever passed statistics class in college. And believe me, I tried—like three times. I have read the stats that say Christianity has been on the decline for decades. For example, in 2020 Barna Research published a report stating that only one in four Americans is a practicing Christian.[1] We may not even need to read studies like that, because we can feel and see it happening. Many of us long for a much-needed revival and awakening.

Year after year, we are gaining some but losing a bunch. So

what is our problem? How are we identified? How do people look at us? What do people think about us? These are all questions I would certainly ask about my business. Especially if we were not growing. But we usually don't think about the whole church around the world. We think about our own little group, about the buildings we sit in on Sunday.

Personally, I think we screwed up most of it. When I say we, I mean humans. Our ways are just not like God's ways and plans (Isaiah 55:8–9). We fall in love with our traditions. We water down the Bible a little bit here and a little bit there. The Christian umbrella seems so big and broad that, at some point, we decided we needed more descriptive "brands" of *our* Christianity. Hence, all the different denominations we have today.

If all this seems confusing to you and me, then imagine how it looks to the world!

But that's actually a big part of the problem. In so many ways it looks *exactly* like the world and its institutions. Our political parties are overcome with infighting. More and more, it is rare when any group, state, county, or even school board can get along or agree on anything. An invitation into the family of God *should* seem different from anything else people have seen or been a part of in their lives.

Consider the whole notion of what we think of as "church." In Matthew 16:18, Jesus said He would build His church from His followers. Well, again, that was *way* too broad for us. So we tweaked it. Church became a certain place we go to for a certain time. We say to invite your friends so they can check it out and maybe even join. Join *this* church, in *this* building. Yet the church of Jesus Christ is way bigger than our buildings—no matter how big they are!

Before you start gathering stones to chuck my way, please hear me out. I love meeting on Sunday mornings with other believers. Because we had a TV show, I now get asked to speak all over the world, and I get to be in many different places full of believers all the time. When I'm home, I also meet locally with a group of believers. Thanks to the internet, I can watch different pastors and Christian communicators all over the world from anywhere I am.

What groups of believers do on Sunday mornings is vital for their lives. Believers meeting together helps us stay strong and dedicated to our Lord. Hopefully, we get fed some spiritual truth and our children are being taught from God's Word during this time. We worship God with our songs and hymns. We collect money to support ministries, which is a practice shown all throughout the New Testament. In fact, meeting on the first day of the week was not our idea but God's. So it's good!

However, when we all get in our buildings and see others in different buildings as not being like us, it can create major disunity. In Martin Luther King Jr.'s famous message titled "Hospitality, Loving Thy Neighbor and Welcoming the Stranger," he stated, "I think it is one of the tragedies of our nation, one of the shameful tragedies, that 11 o'clock on Sunday morning is one of the most segregated hours, if not the most segregated hour in Christian America."[2] Hopefully that has changed some since he said this, but I don't believe it has changed enough. On my ten-minute drive to work, I pass *eight* different church buildings! Now don't get me wrong, I'm happy we have a lot of churches and believers where I live. But we do have a problem if we don't see all those churches as belonging to the global church—the body of Christ. I often wonder why we, as a worldwide group of believers, seem to do much of life inside our own little groups.

The reason I bring all this up is because, with the obvious downward spiral of the culture, what we are doing does not seem to be working. The world seems to be getting darker and darker, while we, as a community of believers, seem to be shrinking. After the book of Acts, did the Good News change? Is the Bible out of touch with our modern society? I don't think so. So it must be us.

There could be several reasons we're shrinking. One is, as believers, we are simply *not* sharing the Good News with people. Perhaps our society has led us to keep more to ourselves and our own problems. It could be a major sin issue, because sin seems to be flaunted everywhere now without an ounce of shame or embarrassment. Have you watched primetime TV lately?

Maybe it's tied to how we *think* about our churches. Perhaps we think that our pastors are the ones tasked with keeping the movement of Jesus going. Our hour or so meeting together each week is supposed to keep us interested, take care of our children, be exciting, be entertaining, and feed us the Word for our upcoming week. Oh yeah, and save all the lost people. *Come on, pastors, that's why we throw money into a plate. Isn't that how it works?*

What if the millions and millions of believers decided to get serious about telling the Good News to all the folks around them?

What if we lived our lives in such a way that they were distinctly different from what others see in the world?

What if we actually used our gifts and skills to do the work so many of us think we just pay pastors and church leaders to do?

If the church ever got together and gave the same efforts we give to our jobs, careers, hobbies, or downtime, it would start changing the world instantly.

Let's take a look at how this whole church concept got going and see if it matches how we live our lives now. Does the life these first believers lived resemble ours today and our mission? Does this look like our churches? If it does, that's fantastic. If not, let's see if we can figure out how to make some changes.

HISTORY MAKERS AND WORLD CHANGERS

In Acts chapter 1, we see Jesus ascending into heaven. He was telling the people to wait for the gift of the Holy Spirit. We also have Peter guiding the disciples as they replaced Judas. The same one who denied Jesus was leading the charge to get the Gospel out. In verse 17, he mentioned that Judas "shared in our ministry," and then he stated that they needed someone to "take over this apostolic ministry" (v. 25). This was an initial move to make sure the Good News was preached to as many as possible.

In chapter 2, after the Holy Spirit roared in, Peter got up and preached the Gospel for the first time, and three thousand responded to the call. The church was formed. They listened to teaching, ate together, and shared their possessions, all while praising God. This was the result: "The Lord added to their number daily those who were being saved" (v. 47).

In chapter 3, we find Peter and John healing people and preaching the Gospel to all who would listen. Chapter 4 is when trouble began. The religious leaders did not like the message about Jesus coming back from the dead. Peter and John getting thrown in jail would become a recurring theme. Even still, more and more were hearing and believing the Gospel and being saved.

Peter and John were asked point-blank by the folks who

jailed them, "Where is all this coming from?" Peter boldly let them know the Gospel message. We've looked at it before, but Acts 4:13 is remarkable to me in so many ways:

> When they saw the courage of Peter and John and realized that they were unschooled, ordinary men, they were astonished and they took note that these men had been with Jesus.

"Unschooled, ordinary men." Sometimes we think that only the highly educated or seminary trained can share about Jesus. We often think of Peter and John as highly trained people simply because they're in the Bible. But that's not how they were seen in that community. They were nothing special. Yet they were noticed because everyone saw their courage. This proves that *how* we share the Gospel can impact people. When we are really fired up about something, people take notice.

The emphasis here is to not believe the lie that you can't speak up because of a lack of formal training. Peter and John sure didn't!

After they were told to shut it down, they responded, "Which is right in God's eyes: to listen to you, or to him? You be the judges! As for us, we cannot help speaking about what we have seen and heard" (Acts 4:19–20).

Would we have this same boldness? Today, can we not help but talk about Jesus?

Next, they prayed to God. Not to protect them from harm. Not to keep them safe. Not to give them a place where they wouldn't have any interference of their freedom of religion. No, they prayed for even more boldness.

"Now, Lord, consider their threats and enable your servants to speak your word with great boldness. Stretch out your hand to heal and perform signs and wonders through the name of your holy servant Jesus." After they prayed, the place where they were meeting was shaken. And they were all filled with the Holy Spirit and spoke the word of God boldly. (vv. 29–31)

The church kept getting stronger and sharing all they had with one another. Acts 5 begins with an odd story of a couple named Ananias and Sapphira who lied to the Holy Spirit and wound up dead. Weird story, for sure. Obviously, this scared everyone. But that fear still didn't stop the Gospel. It kept going. People were getting arrested and threatened, and folks were dying, but the Gospel just kept spreading. "Nevertheless, more and more men and women believed in the Lord and were added to their number" (Acts 5:14).

Now the super religious people were jealous. Peter and the apostles were put back in jail once again. But then an angel let them out. So they ran out of town, right? Nope. They went right back to telling people about Jesus.

Then the high priest and all his associates, who were members of the party of the Sadducees, were filled with jealousy. They arrested the apostles and put them in the public jail. But during the night an angel of the Lord opened the doors of the jail and brought them out. "Go, stand in the temple courts," he said, "and tell the people all about this new life." At daybreak they entered the temple courts, as they had been told, and began to teach the people. (Acts 5:17–21)

When they were brought back in for questioning from the religious leaders about why they wouldn't stop teaching in Jesus' name, Peter's answer was epic:

"We must obey God rather than human beings! The God of our ancestors raised Jesus from the dead—whom you killed by hanging him on a cross. God exalted him to his own right hand as Prince and Savior that he might bring Israel to repentance and forgive their sins. We are witnesses of these things, and so is the Holy Spirit, whom God has given to those who obey him." (vv. 29–32)

I can just see the mic drop now! The leaders were really mad and decided they were just going to kill them. It wasn't really a stretch since they had recently put Jesus to death. (Sort of.) Now, don't think that Peter and his group didn't realize that they were close to their own earthly demise. But that didn't matter, because these guys couldn't care less what the "authorities" told them. They were on a mission!

A guy named Gamaliel calmed everyone down and convinced the other leaders to let them go. He actually had a great theory about what would happen. He had seen people with wild stories come and go. He had seen troublemakers before. Here's what convinced them to let the apostles go:

"Therefore, in the present case I advise you: Leave these men alone! Let them go! For if their purpose or activity is of human origin, it will fail. But if it is from God, you will not be able to stop these men; you will only find yourselves fighting against God." (vv. 38–39)

Wow! He was right. We are still talking about it today! It's not just some weird coincidence. All this was from God. Then they flogged them, or as we said growing up, *they beat the fire outta them.* Okay, surely once they were beaten, they stopped talking about Jesus, right? Nope. They just kept telling people.

The apostles left the Sanhedrin, rejoicing because they had been counted worthy of suffering disgrace for the Name. Day after day, in the temple courts and from house to house, they never stopped teaching and proclaiming the good news that Jesus is the Messiah. (vv. 41–42)

Imagine being grateful for suffering for Jesus! With that mindset, no wonder nothing could stop them from being Gospelers!

THE SEVEN

Then, in Acts chapter 6, another amazing thing happened. We see an intentional move to make sure spreading the Gospel stayed a top priority. An issue came up within the church when some widows were not getting their needs met. Taking care of widows and orphans is what James 1:27 describes as religion that is pure and faultless, so this is an important function of the church. Even today there are people in church groups who sometimes have to let the leaders know they're not happy with how things are going.

So when our priorities are challenged, what is the main thing we're trying to accomplish? Is it sharing our faith with the lost or taking care of all the ones who have obeyed the Gospel? Both are important. Is it possible to be good at both? I believe we have the same challenge today.

Look at what took place:

In those days when the number of disciples was increasing, the Hellenistic Jews among them complained against the Hebraic Jews because their widows were being overlooked in the daily distribution of food. So the Twelve gathered all the disciples together and said, "It would not be right for us to neglect the ministry of the word of God in order to wait on tables. Brothers and sisters, choose seven men from among you who are known to be full of the Spirit and wisdom. We will turn this responsibility over to them and will give our attention to prayer and the ministry of the word."

This proposal pleased the whole group. They chose Stephen, a man full of faith and of the Holy Spirit; also Philip, Procorus, Nicanor, Timon, Parmenas, and Nicolas from Antioch, a convert to Judaism. They presented these men to the apostles, who prayed and laid their hands on them.

So the word of God spread. The number of disciples in Jerusalem increased rapidly, and a large number of priests became obedient to the faith. (Acts 6:1–7)

So the Twelve gathered and decided to choose seven men "full of the Spirit and wisdom." What they were chosen to do is up for debate, one that's been going on for nearly two thousand years. Many say this is where the deacon ministry began. For me personally in my own Bible study, I don't believe that to be the case.

I believe there are deacons who do great work in the church. I just don't think that's what these particular guys were. As we keep reading in the Scriptures, notice what happens to these men. They were not just guys who preached the Gospel; they went to another level.

Look again at verse 7: "So the word of God spread. The number of disciples in Jerusalem increased rapidly, and a large number of priests became obedient to the faith." This is the key point here. The apostles made a move to ensure the church did not become all about itself and forget there's a lost world out there that needs Jesus.

Of course, serving others in our church groups is part of any ministry. It's not a bad thing at all. But if we are not careful, we end up focusing only on the needs of the people in the building and forget there are many more in our communities who have no idea there's another way of life: a way to live with a purpose; a way to have a whole new family to help; a way to have eternal life.

Maybe you never noticed or never knew there was a group that was chosen and given a name—the Seven. I had never heard much about this before either, but I think this passage is a big reminder to everyone who would come after to remember to keep getting the message out.

Stephen was the first named of the Seven. Chapter 6 concludes with him preaching and then being seized and brought before the religious hierarchy. Here, we see the trend continue. What's amazing is what verse 10 says about him: "But they could not stand up against the wisdom the Spirit gave him as he spoke."

In chapter 7, Stephen displayed his gift for speaking the Word of the Lord. He covered Jewish history—Abraham, Isaac, Jacob, Joseph, Moses, Joshua, David—and then closed with Jesus. There was no doubt why Stephen was chosen as one of the

Seven to spread the Good News. He concluded with letting them know they were not right with God.

> You stiff-necked people! Your hearts and ears are still uncir-
> cumcised. You are just like your ancestors: You always resist
> the Holy Spirit! Was there ever a prophet your ancestors did
> not persecute? They even killed those who predicted the com-
> ing of the Righteous One. And now you have betrayed and
> murdered him—you who have received the law that was given
> through angels but have not obeyed it. (vv. 51–53)

He was giving it to them straight. No punches pulled. And so, chapter 7 ends tragically for the first member of the Seven. The people were furious and gnashed their teeth at Stephen. They covered their ears and yelled at the top of their lungs. Then they did the unthinkable and threw stones at him until he died. Stephen, like Jesus, the One he was dying for, asked God to forgive the people killing him.

Surely that had to stop this whole movement, right? Not at all. But it did start a great persecution against all Christians. Next we read about Philip, the second member on the list of the Seven. Philip and many others from the church scattered all over the region. Yet they did not stay silent. They hammered out the message about Jesus. "Those who had been scattered preached the word wherever they went. Philip went down to a city in Samaria and proclaimed the Messiah there" (Acts 8:4–5).

Philip was led to an Ethiopian who had gone to Jerusalem to worship and was returning home in his chariot, reading the scroll (book) of Isaiah.

Now an angel of the Lord said to Philip, "Go south to the road—the desert road—that goes down from Jerusalem to Gaza." So he started out, and on his way he met an Ethiopian eunuch, an important official in charge of all the treasury of the Kandake (which means "queen of the Ethiopians"). This man had gone to Jerusalem to worship, and on his way home was sitting in his chariot reading the Book of Isaiah the prophet. The Spirit told Philip, "Go to that chariot and stay near it." (vv. 26–29)

This is another time where I probably would have misread the situation. This guy looked like he was fired up for the Lord. He had just gone to worship and then he was reading the Bible. I would have just said, "Hey brother, looks like we're on the same team!" But Philip didn't do that. He did what we all need to remember to do—ask questions.

Then Philip ran up to the chariot and heard the man reading Isaiah the prophet. "Do you understand what you are reading?" Philip asked. "How can I," he said, "unless someone explains it to me?" So he invited Philip to come up and sit with him. (vv. 30–31)

There is a great lesson here for us as Gospelers. Don't *assume* people know the Lord. When you ask questions like, "Do you go to church?" and hear, "Yes," don't let that be the end of it. Ask better questions. Get specific. Sometimes, as it turned out for this guy, people need someone to explain it to them. Our job is to be ready when those moments happen.

This is the passage of Scripture the eunuch was reading: "He was led like a sheep to the slaughter, and as a lamb before its shearer is silent, so he did not open his mouth. In his humiliation he was deprived of justice. Who can speak of his descendants? For his life was taken from the earth." The eunuch asked Philip, "Tell me, please, who is the prophet talking about, himself or someone else?" Then Philip began with that very passage of Scripture and told him the good news about Jesus. (vv. 32–35)

All these people we read about knew the Word. I'm grateful Philip did so that he could explain it. This is exactly why we must dive in and study the Bible. Too often, we think that studying Scripture is just to help ourselves, but it can unlock some answers for other people as well—people you may not even know yet.

As they traveled along the road, they came to some water and the eunuch said, "Look, here is water. What can stand in the way of my being baptized?" And he gave orders to stop the chariot. Then both Philip and the eunuch went down into the water and Philip baptized him. When they came up out of the water, the Spirit of the Lord suddenly took Philip away, and the eunuch did not see him again, but went on his way rejoicing. Philip, however, appeared at Azotus and traveled about, preaching the gospel in all the towns until he reached Caesarea. (vv. 36–40)

Once again, we see these guys in the book of Acts go all the way with people to start their new journey with Jesus. This man just needed someone to explain what he was searching for.

Because of Philip's obedience, the eunuch ended up a wet guy traveling back to his home country with a firm understanding of the Gospel.

In studying this story, I did a little research on Ethiopia. Today, the largest religion there is Christianity, where 63 percent of the 113 million people claim to be believers in Jesus Christ. That is a giant group! I also ran across an article from a 2019 edition of *Smithsonian* magazine that reported, "In the dusty highlands of northern Ethiopia, a team of archaeologists recently uncovered the oldest known Christian church in sub-Saharan Africa, a find that sheds new light on one of the Old World's most enigmatic kingdoms—and its surprisingly early conversion to Christianity."[3]

This story in the book of Acts may very well be where it all started for this whole country—with Philip, one of the Seven, sent out to share the Gospel. He was led to a guy he had never met who seemed to be a believer but didn't know what he was reading. Philip answered his questions, which changed the Ethiopian's life forever and the history of millions of others in his home country, as is evidenced today.

STEP UP AND SPEAK UP

That reminds me of those worms I used to search for when I was a young "retailer." You gotta keep pulling the leaves back and looking for them. When the soil is the right condition, they are there for the taking, even though the exposure and the light make some try to take off. But that never stopped me. As a kid, I learned to love finding those worms. In fact, even today you might catch me down by a pond or river still scratching back the leaves looking for some (even though they're not for sale).

In my opening stories about my worm farm and candy business as a budding retailer and entrepreneur, I wanted to show you how God has used my personal drive and gifting. The reason I'm not shy about sharing Jesus with anyone is because I feel like I have the greatest gift in the world to offer people. Whatever your skills, talents, and history might be, that unique mix can be used in spreading the word about Jesus too.

The word *retail* actually means "to sell in small quantities directly to the ultimate consumer."[4] The Gospel is best delivered one personal conversation at a time (small quantities) to those in need of salvation (the ultimate consumer), knowing that God does the work and drives the message home. We just need to be obedient to have the conversation. These stories we've walked through, like Philip and the eunuch, should inspire us today to step up and speak up in our own conversations with all those we talk to, for those who need their darkness to turn to light.

As we read on in the Bible, we never hear anything about the other five of the Seven. Yet we have to assume the first two, Stephen and Philip, were not the exceptions and that the others were just as influential in the life of the early church and spread of the Gospel. Right off the bat, we know Stephen died for what he believed, becoming a martyr. Later, we catch back up with Philip in Acts 21:8, where Paul talked about meeting him. "Leaving the next day, we reached Caesarea and stayed at the house of Philip the evangelist, one of the Seven."

Notice it states, "Philip the evangelist, one of the Seven." This was a group of evangelists—Gospelers! It's crazy to think that Paul, at that time known as Saul, had been an ally of the religious leaders and cheering on the death of Stephen. His amazing transformation took place during the absolute strangest conversation in the book of Acts, which we'll look at next. But that's exactly what the Gospel can do by making something happen that everyone believes to be impossible. Kind of like a poor kid on the river selling worms for a nickel who ends up helping his family sell millions of duck calls after being on a reality TV show. You just can't make this stuff up!

> Jesus looked at them intently and said, "Humanly speaking, it is impossible. But with God everything is possible." (Matthew 19:26 NLT)

Ten

HOPE YELLER

RUCK WAS A DRUG DEALER IN HOUSTON, TEXAS. HE HAD A VERY ROUGH childhood, never knew his father, and was raised by his mother and grandmother. When he was just a kid, their house burned to the ground. With no money or insurance and nowhere else to go, they just kept living in the burned-out structure. At only nine years old, Ruck witnessed his first murder. By eleven, he started using marijuana and then began selling. The following year at age twelve, he joined a gang and became a crack dealer.

When Ruck was thirteen, his mom passed away. That same year, he got his first gun and committed armed robbery. He was arrested, convicted, and sent to a youth prison in Texas. Three years later, at the age of sixteen, Ruck was released. With nowhere to go and no hope, once again, he returned to all he knew—selling drugs. But this time he got in deeper, running drugs from Texas all the way to the East Coast.

After a deal went bad, he was arrested again, but this time for murder. The chance of spending most if not all of his life behind bars was a real possibility. His friend, who was already looking at a life sentence, wrote a letter to the district attorney confessing to the murder. The friend's story freed Ruck, giving him the unthinkable—another chance at life.

But after his release, Ruck went right back to his old tricks on the streets. After a fling with a girlfriend, they had a son. When he thought a move away from Houston might be a good idea, he soon found out that a change of scenery was not enough to change him. After moving to East Texas, he was still doing the only job he knew—dealing drugs. With all he had been through in his young life, getting drunk and high became his only coping skills. Ruck had *no* belief in God whatsoever.

When his grandmother, who was in bad health, decided to move to Monroe, Louisiana, Ruck agreed to move there to help her. Trying to find something in life that could be positive, he decided to get a real job in this new town where no one knew him. Maybe he could even turn his life around. But after applying at every fast-food joint, he got no callbacks. It's not easy getting a job once you have a record, not even at a drive-thru. Once again, becoming a dealer looked like his only option. No matter where Ruck went, there always seemed to be a demand for drugs, and the one thing he knew how to do well was supply.

But he decided on one last shot, trying to get a job at an odd place. A big ol' warehouse that sold duck calls. Yep, Duck Commander got an application from the guy with a checkered past. He was surprised when he got a call from one of our managers asking him to come in for an interview. The good news was Ruck was hired. But he had no idea that he was getting ready to hear some even better news.

His first job was folding T-shirts, but Ruck eventually worked his way up in the company. He even landed on an episode of *Duck*

Dynasty. After the guys at work started bringing him to Bible studies and church, Ruck gave his life to the Lord in 2014, washing away the past that had so much sin and tragedy. After having been dealt a tough hand in life and then blowing every chance, now, finally, he was made new by the blood of Jesus Christ.

Ruck found hope.

In the beginning, he still had his ups and downs. Just like I always heard growing up, "You might be done with sin, but that doesn't mean sin is done with you!" There are earthly consequences from the past that we all will have to deal with, but if you have the Spirit, you have help to guide and carry you through them. Over the past few years, Ruck and I have spent a whole lot of time talking about what it really means to live for Jesus.

Even when Ruck had given up on himself, God never gave up on him. When there seemed to be no hope to be found anywhere, he ran into a bunch of guys who didn't define him by his past. Ruck ran into some hope yellers!

His story reminds me of when we talked about Peter's major fail when he denied knowing his Friend, Companion, and Lord. Even after those mistakes, Jesus offered him hope. We may not verbally deny Jesus, but at times our actions can sure look as if we don't know him. The truth is we've all had terrible things happen in our past. Peter's story is really no different from ours. Ruck's story is really no different from ours.

ANYONE CAN CHANGE

At the end of the last chapter, I referred to a very strange conversation documented in the book of Acts. That story is about a guy whose past was unmatched by most folks. He was a murderer. And his motivation to kill is unthinkable in our country—murdering anyone who speaks out about Jesus Christ. That is a whole other realm of evil.

In Acts chapter 7, Stephen had preached a Gospel sermon to the Sanhedrin court. He ended with the accusation that they had killed everyone who predicted the Messiah would come, including the Messiah Himself. That's when things turned violent.

When the members of the Sanhedrin heard this, they were furious and gnashed their teeth at him. But Stephen, full of the Holy Spirit, looked up to heaven and saw the glory of God, and Jesus standing at the right hand of God. "Look," he said, "I see heaven open and the Son of Man standing at the right hand of God." At this they covered their ears and, yelling at the top of their voices, they all rushed at him, dragged him out of the city and began to stone him. (vv. 54–58)

The nature of Stephen's death makes you wonder how humans could be so awful and cruel. To think that he was being killed for trying to spread the Gospel is mind-blowing. In a senseless execution committed by ruthless, "religious" people, Stephen became one of the first of many Gospelers who would be cut down. Sadly, today, believers all over the world are still being persecuted and punished for their faith in Christ.

In the second part of verse 58, we are introduced to a young man who was there watching when Stephen was being stoned to death: "Meanwhile, the witnesses laid their coats at the feet of a young man named Saul."

This is the first mention of this guy named Saul. But if we

fast-forward to Acts 22, he told us exactly what he was doing there when Stephen died.

> "'Lord,' I replied, 'these people know that I went from one synagogue to another to imprison and beat those who believe in you. And when the blood of your martyr Stephen was shed, I stood there giving my approval and guarding the clothes of those who were killing him.'" (vv. 19–20)

Just like Ruck's crime buddy, Saul made a full confession here. Because he was a bad guy indeed, he would need something big to happen to get his attention. There seemed to be little hope for someone like him. It reminds me in a way of what people probably thought about my father. *How would he ever change?* But that's the best part of the Gospel and why I love it so much. There is *always* hope! Hope for people we would never dream could change. For anyone who knew him, Saul was, for sure, one of those.

> Meanwhile, Saul was still breathing out murderous threats against the Lord's disciples. He went to the high priest and asked him for letters to the synagogues in Damascus, so that if he found any there who belonged to the Way, whether men or women, he might take them as prisoners to Jerusalem. (Acts 9:1–2)

You have to look at someone like Saul and try to imagine what their life would look like if they loved the Lord. No matter how bad it looks now, what if they turned all of their passion for the things of this world to passion for God? We have to remember that with the Gospel, *anyone* can change. God's power and message are for us, even the *worst* of us. Our only hope is getting Light into the darkness.

For Saul, God did something extraordinary. He let him have an encounter with Jesus, literally. But since Jesus had already ascended into heaven, this was the "aerial version"

> WITH THE GOSPEL, *ANYONE* CAN CHANGE. GOD'S POWER AND MESSAGE ARE FOR US, EVEN THE *WORST* OF US.

of Christ. Sometimes God does some unusual things to get people's attention. I have talked to a few folks who know God has called them to Him, even when no one directly shared with them. Their past crashed into Jesus, just like Saul's was about to do.

> As he neared Damascus on his journey, suddenly a light from heaven flashed around him. He fell to the ground and heard a voice say to him, "Saul, Saul, why do you persecute me?" "Who are you, Lord?" Saul asked. "I am Jesus, whom you are persecuting," he replied. "Now get up and go into the city, and you will be told what you must do." (vv. 3–6)

Saul was doing some of the worst things ever against the church that Christ formed, and he had *no* desire to change. But then everything transformed when he had a conversation with Jesus Himself, who is described here as being a powerful Light, taking over all the darkness in Saul's life. He even referred to Jesus as Lord.

When we encounter Jesus and see the Light that He is, that should cause a change in us. He is so bright that everything about this life should come into clear focus. We should be able to see very plainly that we are obviously not in control and, as Lord, He is. Saul was now ready to go do whatever it was this Light named Jesus told him to do! Talk about a wild conversion.

> The men traveling with Saul stood there speechless; they heard the sound but did not see anyone. Saul got up from the ground, but when he opened his eyes he could see nothing. So they led him by the hand into Damascus. For three days he was blind, and did not eat or drink anything. (vv. 7–9)

So many of us have to hit rock bottom before we realize how much we need God, but this was a whole new level. It's hard to know exactly what Saul was thinking during this encounter. Being blinded and then not eating or drinking allowed him to relive the conversation he had with Jesus. When our sins come out into the light, they have a way of making our spiritual vision clear. This was happening with Saul, even in his blindness. However, Jesus would not leave him in that state. He would give him hope.

BECOMING A MESSENGER

In Damascus there was a disciple named Ananias. The Lord called to him in a vision, "Ananias!"

"Yes, Lord," he answered.

The Lord told him, "Go to the house of Judas on Straight Street and ask for a man from Tarsus named Saul, for he is praying. In a vision he has seen a man named Ananias come and place his hands on him to restore his sight."

"Lord," Ananias answered, "I have heard many reports about this man and all the harm he has done to your holy people in Jerusalem. And he has come here with authority from the chief priests to arrest all who call on your name." (vv. 10–14)

Don't you just love getting dragged into other people's problems? Well, my hope is to try to get you to do just that—help others. Just like Jesus told Ananias to go and help people who had messed up their lives, He wants us to do the same. If that part of being a Gospeler does not sit well with you, you need to remember that Jesus did the same for you and me. He did not *have* to come to earth; He *chose* to.

I know you may be thinking right now, *So, Willie, you're saying that even though I have chosen to do all these things right, now I have to mess with people who live their lives in a stupid and selfish way? Why am I the one who has to deal to them? You expect me to take time out of my busy schedule to help these types of people?*

Well, yes. In fact, Jesus led the way. When we didn't know Him, we all did stupid and selfish things. Kind of like our own children do. We don't tell our kids that because we don't act like children anymore, we're not going to help them any longer. No. We help them *because* we know we were children at one time. We're just much further down the road and know what to do. That's the reason we're the *best* ones to help them.

Ananias was about to play a crucial role in a new Gospel

genealogy. But he had no idea he was being hesitant to help someone who would impact the rest of humanity for centuries. He did not even realize the plan God had for Saul in his lifetime. But the world would come to know this man as Paul, the apostle who would leave his mark on both the kingdom and the world in a huge way. Ananias would help him get started.

> But the Lord said to Ananias, "Go! This man is my chosen instrument to proclaim my name to the Gentiles and their kings and to the people of Israel. I will show him how much he must suffer for my name." Then Ananias went to the house and entered it. Placing his hands on Saul, he said, "Brother Saul, the Lord—Jesus, who appeared to you on the road as you were coming here—has sent me so that you may see again and be filled with the Holy Spirit." Immediately, something like scales fell from Saul's eyes, and he could see again. He got up and was baptized, and after taking some food, he regained his strength. (vv. 15–19)

Even though he absolutely wanted no part in it at first, Ananias did exactly as he was told and helped this guy. He was there when Saul received the Holy Spirit. He was there when Saul was baptized. Can you imagine the story Ananias had for his friends? Can you imagine how the whole church who lived in fear of this guy must have felt when they learned that Saul had been baptized, just like they had been?

WE DON'T ALWAYS KNOW OR UNDERSTAND THE PLANS GOD HAS FOR US.

We don't always know or understand the plans God has for us. So, sometimes, we have to be nudged. Especially when it comes to dealing with other people—that can be frightening. What is even crazier is we have no idea the plans God has for all these people after they obey the Gospel, after we share the Good News with them. We have no idea how many future lives will be impacted. All we know is that we are involved with helping to start a story that God will keep writing.

God also had a plan for Saul to be one of the first to take the Gospel to the Gentile world. He knew that some would have a unique ability to get the message to certain people. Saul was one of those. Many of us should be really happy for this, because we are fellow Gentiles. We know the Gospel today because of this very story!

God had a specific plan for Paul to preach the Gospel to the Gentiles. Ruck has been able to share with people who have a similar past as him. So who are those folks who might be moved by your story and hear the Gospel through it? Who are the people your pastor, or I, or anyone else may not be able to reach quite like you can?

Saul-who-was-also-called-Paul's story should always be a reminder to us that *no one* is too far gone to make a drastic life change when they encounter Jesus. No matter how bad someone may be, there is *always* hope. There is that slight crack where some light can get in and start clearing out the darkness.

We can't just give up on certain people, assuming they will never respond. Or worse, not even try. My aunt Jan didn't give up on my dad. If everyone had given up hope for my parents, I might not be writing this book now. I always remember that truth when I encounter people. Just like Pastor Bill took a chance on my dad, I can take a chance on someone others may have given up on.

I know I could help change someone's family forever, just like mine was changed. The lives of our children have been changed because Korie and I accepted the Gospel, and we pray that will go on and on through generations to come.

The world without Jesus is dark and filled with cruelty, pain, and death. But it's dark only because there is no light there. We don't get mad at a dark room just because there's no light. Instead, we have to focus on how to get light into that room. Whether we use electricity, a flashlight, or light a candle, we know there are ways to bring light into darkness. And there are always ways to bring the Gospel into a dark world.

Preaching the Past

I know the world looks really bleak these days. We hear many people even use the word *hopeless* to describe its condition. Just as I'm sure you do, I see and hear the pain and suffering all around us. While, yes, it is bad now, there has always been darkness in this life. I often hear folks calling for us to go back to living the way people did in the past. Their idea is that there was a time when things seemed more godly or holy. Hearing them talk, it's almost as if life was great back in the "good ol' days" and then, at some point, everything went wrong.

When we try to return to something we created, rather than the Creator, we are simply focusing on the imperfect as opposed to the Perfect. Every society or philosophy that has some good in it, even some form of godliness, has always included evil and injustice. No matter how much humans try to get it right, we seem to always get it wrong. Whether we're looking at the past or the present, that's been proven without a doubt.

The United States is such a great example. We may hear a

message preached that we need to go back to when we think this country was better. But how far back do you want to go? When people were being enslaved? When we had a civil war and killed our own countrymen? When children worked in coal mines? When civil rights were not for all? When women couldn't even vote? So is going back really the best option? When you "go back," you have to take the bad with the good. And some of it was *really* bad.

I believe we need to go back, alright, but not to something we created. We need to go back to what God reveals in the Bible through Jesus Christ. As Paul wrote,

> But one thing I do: Forgetting what is behind and straining toward what is ahead, I press on toward the goal to win the prize for which God has called me heavenward in Christ Jesus. (Philippians 3:13–14)

Great advice. Let's press on too. We've got a future ahead, and we can't get stuck in the past.

Preaching the Darkness

There is certainly darkness all around us today. It seems like many believers think they have been called to shout out how dark the world is rather than proclaim hope for all the ones trapped in it. So many Christians seem to enjoy telling each other how bad the world has become. We tweet, post, debate, and discuss it. It's like we all bring our candles inside our buildings of worship and say, "Well, thank God it's not dark in here." Much like the Pharisee's prayer that Jesus warned us to stay clear of in Luke 18:11: "God, I thank you that I am not like other people—robbers, evildoers, adulterers—or even like this tax collector."

But Jesus told His disciples to go! Not go to church. Not go for safety. Not go and tell everyone how bad the world is. If you have become a person who never tries to share the Gospel with anyone but constantly rants about how this country is going to hell in a handbasket, then you need a reminder of where Jesus told *His people* to go. Go into the darkness with light, and be a hope yeller.

If most of this world may be headed to hell, then the real question is, What are we doing about it? Telling everyone you know that everything is screwed up is not really going to solve the problem. Telling everyone you know about the One who came to fix the problem of sin will.

It reminds me of a rule I have at our office: don't bring me a problem without a solution. It makes my employees think before they complain—because complaints turn into negativity, but solutions turn into action.

Jesus told us that, because of Him, we are lights *in* the world and *to* the world, so being light should be our focus.

> "You are the light of the world. A town built on a hill cannot be hidden. Neither do people light a lamp and put it under a bowl. Instead they put it on its stand, and it gives light to everyone in the house." (Matthew 5:14–15)

Preaching the Government

Some of us make things sound like the Gospel is not the real solution anymore. We speak as if the government is the only thing that will get us back in good shape. We start to think if we can just get "the right people" in office who "believe like we believe," then surely we can be a godly nation. Well, if you believe that, you certainly believe more in the government than I do.

I'm not saying we can't vote for good people who have faith. We should. But for real change to happen, those of us in the church of Jesus have to do the job our Commander told us to do. Jesus didn't talk about changing the system so His believers' calling would be easy. If that were the playbook, I think He would have let us know. So if you constantly spout political news, you are probably not a hope yeller.

One truth we have proven over centuries is that laws will not make people Christlike. Even the Old Testament shows us that.

> But the plans of the LORD stand firm forever, the purposes of his heart through all generations.
> Blessed is the nation whose God is the LORD, the people he chose for his inheritance. (Psalm 33:11–12)

Preaching to the Choir

As Christians, we are yelling alright, but not yelling hope—it's more like we're screaming despair. It seems like our mission is to let everyone know how bad things are going in the world. But I'm not sure the world is even hearing it. Jesus never told us this was our mission. In fact, He said to not be surprised when people in the world act the way they do. It's amazing to me that too often we do exactly what Jesus said we shouldn't—act surprised.

> "If the world hates you, keep in mind that it hated me first. If you belonged to the world, it would love you as its own. As it is, you do not belong to the world, but I have chosen you out of the world. That is why the world hates you." (John 15:18–19)

Jesus plainly tells us how we should approach the world:

"For God so loved the world that he gave his one and only Son, that whoever believes in him shall not perish but have eternal life. For God did not send his Son into the world to condemn the world, but to save the world through him." (John 3:16–17)

When we preach to the choir, it can sure sound like we are simply trying to condemn the world rather than offer hope and the truth that we know there is a better way. It's like we forget the world is full of people who are just like we were at one time. And, as people who are still sinners, we sometimes find ourselves dipping back into the same old stuff that looks like the world.

I have heard believers who think our actions should resemble the time Jesus turned over the tables and drove some folks out of the temple. The claim of "righteous anger" is the fuel that powers their harshness, while they fail to remember that Jesus' toughest words were for the religious people. He turned over the tables in the temple courtyard, not at the bar down the street. The real message of Jesus is that He came for the sick, to set captives free, and He died on the cross for *all* humanity (Isaiah 61 1–2). Jesus asked God to forgive the very people participating in killing Him. He said they had no idea what they were doing (Luke 23:34). That's what we need to be hollering: humble forgiveness that leads to hope.

Now, back to Saul, who changed not only his life but also his name. He became Paul, who went on to write much of the New Testament. He took the message to the Gentiles and to kings and to anyone he could reach. His writings about the testimony he found in Jesus still inspire people thousands of years after he had his conversation with Him on the road to Damascus.

So whatever happened to Ruck? Well, he went on to become an addiction counselor. Today, he leads a giant, vibrant Celebrate Recovery group. He has spoken all over the country, telling not only his story but the story he heard that changed everything for him—the Gospel of Jesus.

God uses folks like Ruck to go after people who may never meet me or you. Ruck's past gives him insight to have the right words to hit home and land the Gospel in their lives. He sees conversations every day that turn dark paths into light—exactly what happened to him.

99/ONE

To be honest, I have certainly been guilty at times of getting caught up in how bad things seem to be going in the world. I was becoming more and more shocked until I finally started *not* being shocked. Seeing and hearing things that once seemed unthinkable in society slowly became the norm. In 2020, during the pandemic, I got to thinking, *Am I just lamenting all the time about society, or am I taking action to try to improve it?* That's when I decided to become more intentional about getting the Gospel out to more people.

I approached my local church staff with ideas to help do just that. Like we saw in Acts 6 with the apostles' intentional creation of the Seven, I threw out ideas to help organize people to focus on sharing the Gospel with others. The church I attend didn't have a specific ministry for this, so I was tasked with getting one started. I began to gather people who could share in this effort in a new ministry that would be called 99/One.

The idea of 99/One was to never forget the truth that Jesus spoke of in the parable of the shepherd who left the ninety-nine sheep to find the *one* that was lost (Matthew 18 and Luke 15). We would meet after each church service to help answer spiritual questions for anyone who came in to visit. As I mentioned in the story about Alyssa, we called our room First Step, for people looking to make a first step toward Jesus. Some came in to do just that, while others came in to learn how to share their faith.

Over the last few years, we have studied the Bible and shared the Gospel with many people. We've also trained a bunch of folks who wanted to get serious about having an answer for the hope they have in Jesus (1 Peter 3:15). Now, for the first time, this church has a specific ministry dedicated to following the Great Commission Jesus challenged us to live by in Matthew 28:18–20.

What I've walked you through in this book is what we do in 99/One. We look at a bunch of scriptures about people in the New Testament who made their first steps toward the Gospel. We cover the basics of repentance, baptism, confessing Christ, and sin. We discuss the Holy Spirit and look for true belief in God and Jesus. Because of our team's efforts, many people have come to know Him.

One of my favorite stories that has come out of 99/One is about Shellie, a woman around my age. She came to our room every time we were there. She would just write the whole time, taking notes. But Shellie never said a word. Eventually, I found out she had found her faith in the Lord a few years prior.

One Sunday morning, I asked Shellie, "Do you ever see your-self presenting the Gospel in this room?"

She quickly fired back, "No way."

I told Shellie that she could indeed share all the information she was learning, and the Holy Spirit would fill in the gaps. Little did she know, about a month later, her chance would come. On Easter Sunday, our church had multiple services. I would have to miss one of them to be at another commitment.

As with most churches, we have more visitors than ever at Easter services. Sadly, it doesn't seem to be a day when we hear of large crowds experiencing repentance and revival. Maybe it's because we focus on the new outfit for the celebration and all the afternoon festivities. Church seems to just be another event on the day's schedule.

So I asked none other than Shellie if she could fill in for me during the time I'd be gone. (She confessed to me later that she felt like throwing up when I asked her to be there to present the Gospel if anyone showed up.)

I came up to the church the night before for a Saturday Easter service and then, afterward, she and I went over everything one last time. Though I believed Shellie was up to the challenge, I was thinking to myself, *No one is going to show up anyway; it's Easter Sunday.* The next morning, I was at the first service and, just as I thought, no one showed up at 99/One. Soon, Shellie came to the room as planned, and I told her I would return in about an hour and a half.

Later, as I was driving back into the church parking lot, I noticed one of our pastors dragging our little baptismal tub out in front of the building. I jumped out of my truck to begin helping him fill it with water.

"So, who's getting baptized?" I asked.

"Oh, a man and his son," he replied.

Surprised and excited, I asked, "Did they come to the 99/One class?"

"They did!"

"Did they talk with Shellie?"

"They sure did!"

Shellie had done something she *never* thought she could do.

Shellie had done something she had even told me she would *never* do.

But on the morning of Resurrection Day, Shellie had a pointed conversation, with not just one but two people, about making their first step toward Jesus. Just a few months before, she couldn't see herself sharing her faith in that way, ever.

Funny thing is, I never had to try to motivate her from that moment on.

Shellie was hooked on sharing Jesus.

Since that Sunday morning, Shellie has gone on to share with many, many others. Every time, she uses her natural gifts as a mother and her life experiences to reach people. She isn't a Bible scholar, nor has she ever worked for a church. But Shellie has found a powerful mission in life that offers hope to a dark world.

Shellie is a hope yeller.

Shellie is a Gospeler.

IT'S YOUR TURN

I see Saul's life as a symbol of a lost and broken world, one that looks impossible to save. But Jesus coming into his life and radically transforming him proves to us He can make *anyone* into a new creation.

My hope and prayer is that in reading about my experiences with folks like Bill, Jake, Charlie, Rick, Ruck, and Shellie, you will become a believer who offers hope to people who desperately need it. This method I use to reach people in conversations is certainly not the only way to share your faith. It's not tied to any particular church, denomination, or group. It is, however, anchored in the New Testament and, for sure, a great place to start.

I want to encourage you to fall in love with the Word of God.

I want to challenge you to ask bold questions about faith in your conversations with others.

I want to inspire you that when other folks see only the bad in people, you'll look for the good that could come if they opened up their hearts to what Jesus can do in their lives.

Let Jesus lead you to become a person known for spreading the Gospel publicly, personally, and privately.

Become a Gospeler.

NOTES

Introduction

1. A Google search brings up a definition of *Gospeler* from the *Oxford Languages Dictionary.*

Chapter 1

1. "New Survey from Ancestry Shows More Than Half of Americans Can't Name All Four Grandparents," Ancestry.com, March 30, 2022, https://www.ancestry.com/corporate/newsroom/press-releases /new-survey-ancestry-shows-more-half-americans-cant-name-all -four.

Chapter 2

1. *Merriam-Webster*, s.v. "impel (v.)," accessed August 27, 2023, https://www.merriam-webster.com/dictionary/impel.

Chapter 3

1. Noam Cohen, "'Duck Dynasty' Season Opens to Record Ratings," *New York Times*, August 15, 2013, https://www.nytimes.com /2013/08/16/business/media/duck-dynasty-season-opens-to-record -ratings.html.

Chapter 5

1. Lee Strobel, *The Case for Christ* (Grand Rapids: Zondervan, 1998), 225.

Chapter 6

1. *Merriam-Webster*, s.v. "repent (v.)," accessed August 28, 2023, https://www.merriam-webster.com/dictionary/repent.

Chapter 7

1. Richard Hollerman, "How Is Baptism Defined by Greek Dictionaries?," Truediscipleship, accessed August 28, 2023, https://truediscipleship.com/how-is-baptism-defined-by -greek-dictionaries-3/.

Chapter 8

1. *Merriam-Webster*, s.v. "interstellar (adj.)," accessed August 28, 2023, https://www.merriam-webster.com/dictionary/interstellar.

Chapter 9

1. "Signs of Decline & Hope Among Key Metrics of Faith," Barna Research, March 4, 2020, https://www.barna.com/research /changing-state-of-the-church/.
2. L. Z. Granderson, "Can America Break Through the Tribalism of Sunday Mornings?," *Los Angeles Times*, February 14, 2021, https://www.latimes .com/opinion/story/2021–02–14/segregation-churches-politics -maverick-city-music.
3. Andrew Lawler, "Church Unearthed in Ethiopia Rewrites the History of Christianity in Africa," *Smithsonian* magazine, December 10, 2019, https://www.smithsonianmag.com/history/church-unearthed-ethiopia -rewrites-history-christianity-africa-180973740/#:~:text=In%20the%20 dusty%20highlands%20of,surprisingly%20early%20conversion%20 to%20Christianity.
4. *Merriam-Webster*, s.v. "retail (v.)," accessed August 28, 2023, https://www.merriam-webster.com/dictionary/retail.

ABOUT THE AUTHOR

WILLIE ROBERTSON IS THE CEO OF DUCK COMMANDER AND BUCK Commander and star of A&E's *Duck Dynasty*. Robertson has expanded his family companies, from a living room operation to a multimillion-dollar enterprise and destination for all things outdoors. Duck Commander is the bestselling duck call brand in the United States. Duck Commander and Buck Commander are popular trademarks on apparel, hunting gear, food items, and more. Robertson is executive producer of A&E's *Duck Dynasty* and the Outdoor Channel's *Buck Commander*. He is a *New York Times* bestselling author of *The Duck Commander Family: How Faith, Family and Ducks Built a Dynasty* as well as *American Hunter, American Fisherman*, and *American Entrepreneur*. Robertson's story is a remarkable example of entrepreneurship and dedication built on hard work, faith, and family.

BASED ON THE INSPIRING TRUE STORY THAT STARTED A DYNASTY

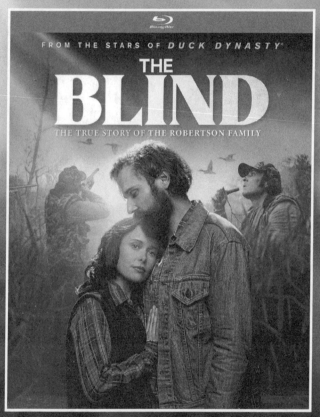

FROM THE STARS OF *DUCK DYNASTY*®

THE BLIND

THE TRUE STORY OF THE ROBERTSON FAMILY

Long before Phil Robertson (*Duck Dynasty*®) became a reality TV star, he fell in love with Miss Kay and started a family, but his demons threatened to tear their lives apart. Set in the backwoods swamps of 1960s Louisiana, THE BLIND shares never-before-revealed moments in Phil's life as he seeks to conquer the shame of his past, ultimately finding redemption in an unlikely place.

AVAILABLE NOW ON BLU-RAY™, DVD AND DIGITAL

Also available wherever books are sold . . .

WILLIE ROBERTSON

SHARING JESUS

WITH CONFIDENCE

How to Be a Gospeler and Have
Conversations that Matter for Eternity

a 64-page Gospeler companion handbook.